Advanced Introduction to Central Bar

Elgar Advanced Introductions are stimulating and thoughtful introductions to major fields in the social sciences, business and law, expertly written by the world's leading scholars. Designed to be accessible yet rigorous, they offer concise and lucid surveys of the substantive and policy issues associated with discrete subject areas.

The aims of the series are two-fold: to pinpoint essential principles of a particular field, and to offer insights that stimulate critical thinking. By distilling the vast and often technical corpus of information on the subject into a concise and meaningful form, the books serve as accessible introductions for undergraduate and graduate students coming to the subject for the first time. Importantly, they also develop well-informed, nuanced critiques of the field that will challenge and extend the understanding of advanced students, scholars and policy-makers.

For a full list of titles in the series, please see the back of the book. Recent titles in the series include:

Marketing Strategy
George S. Day

Business and Human Rights
Peter T. Muchlinski

Scenario Planning
Paul Schoemaker

Spatial Statistics
Daniel A. Griffith and Bin Li

Financial Inclusion
Robert Lensink, Calumn Hamilton and Charles Adjasi

The Sociology of the Self
Shanyang Zhao

Children's Rights
Wouter Vandenhole and Gamze Erdem Türkelli

Artificial Intelligence in Healthcare
Tom Davenport, John Glaser and Elizabeth Gardner

Sustainable Careers
Jeffrey H. Greenhaus and Gerard A. Callanan

Central Banks and Monetary Policy
Jakob de Haan and Christiaan Pattipeilohy

Advanced Introduction to

Central Banks and Monetary Policy

JAKOB DE HAAN

Professor of Political Economy, University of Groningen, the Netherlands

CHRISTIAAN PATTIPEILOHY

Counsellor to the Executive Board of the European Central Bank

Elgar Advanced Introductions

Edward Elgar
PUBLISHING

Cheltenham, UK • Northampton, MA, USA

Published by
Edward Elgar Publishing Limited
The Lypiatts
15 Lansdown Road
Cheltenham
Glos GL50 2JA
UK

Edward Elgar Publishing, Inc.
William Pratt House
9 Dewey Court
Northampton
Massachusetts 01060
USA

A catalogue record for this book
is available from the British Library

Library of Congress Control Number: 2022938916

MIX
Paper from
responsible sources
FSC® C013056

ISBN 978 1 83910 486 2 (cased)
ISBN 978 1 83910 487 9 (eBook)
ISBN 978 1 83910 488 6 (paperback)

Printed and bound in Great Britain by TJ Books Limited, Padstow, Cornwall

Contents

Introduction to *Central Banks and Monetary Policy*

Prior to the 1990s, conventional wisdom among central bankers was that monetary policy-makers should say as little as possible, and say it cryptically. As shown by Alan Blinder (2004), central banking has changed significantly. These changes, Blinder argues, have been sufficiently profound to even constitute a revolution in central banking. Whereas central bankers once believed in secrecy and even mystery, greater openness is now considered a virtue.

Despite greater central bank transparency, central bankers are still often described as mysterious. For instance, a book about the history of the Federal Reserve by William Greider (1989) was called *Secrets of the Temple*. According to the publisher, "This ground-breaking best-seller reveals for the first time how the mighty and mysterious Federal Reserve operates—and how it manipulated and transformed both the American economy and the world's during the last eight crucial years. ... *Secrets of the Temple* takes us inside the government institution that is in some ways more secretive than the CIA and more powerful than the President or Congress." Likewise, the book by Neil Irwin (2013) is entitled: *The Alchemists: Three Central Bankers and a World on Fire*. The book features the leaders of the world's three most important central banks during the Global Financial Crisis and, according to the publisher, "presents the truly global story of the central bankers' role in the world economy that we have been missing."

All this might suggest that the world of central banking is mysterious and hard to understand for outsiders. The authors of this book—economists who have experience in central banking and research on central banking—

beg to differ. The book aims to explain central banking to a non-specialist audience, showing in a non-technical way what central banks do and why.

The book was written in the second half of 2021, but it tries to provide an overview that is both backward- and forward-looking. It offers, for instance, a very brief historical overview of the gestation of central banks, and also discusses ways in which views about monetary policy have evolved. But it also touches upon several challenges that central banks face, not only now but also in the years ahead. It focuses upon the policies of the major central banks in the world, i.e., the Federal Reserve System in the US, the Bank of England and the European Central Bank, but it also provides examples based on central banks elsewhere.

The oldest existing central bank is the Sveriges Riksbank, the central bank of Sweden, which was created in 1668. However, at the time, the bank was not considered a central bank as we know it today. According to Wikipedia, a central bank is "an institution that manages the currency and monetary policy of a state or formal monetary union.[1] ... Most central banks also have supervisory and regulatory powers to ensure the stability of member institutions, to prevent bank runs, and to discourage reckless or fraudulent behaviour by ... banks."[2] As will be explained in Chapter 1, the central banks of the UK, the US and the euro area have a very different historical background. Political interests and the economic problems at the time played a key role in their gestation. This is not unique to these central banks. Often a fiscal motive (think of the need to finance a war) or an attempt to stem (the incidence of) financial crises can explain the creation of a central bank.

Chapter 1 also discusses the organizational design of central banks, showing that, early in their history, most central banks were dominated by a single decision-maker (the governor). Nowadays, most central banks are run by committees. As argued by Blinder (2004), the various reasons to explain this come down, in one way or another, to diversification of risk. Another feature characterizing modern central banks, not only in advanced economies but also in many emerging and developing economies, is their independence from government. The trend towards increasing independent central banks is based on the prevailing consensus among policy-makers and academics, that it leads to superior macroeconomic outcomes, notably lower and more stable inflation. This is important, as nowadays most central banks have price stability as their primary objective. It is widely believed that independent central banks should be accountable. After all, unlike government, central bankers are not elected, and thus cannot be voted out of office if the electorate is not satisfied with their performance. Once the (elected) legislator delegates a particular task to the central bank and gives it instruments to perform this task, the central bank must be held accountable for achieving the objective. This means that the legislator (and the general public) must form an opinion of the central bank's performance. In other words, a central bank should be transparent about its policies.

Chapter 2 shows that most central banks in advanced countries define price stability as an inflation rate around 2 per cent over a specific policy horizon and explains the rationale for these targets. It also shows that many central banks have introduced a particular monetary policy strategy to realize this objective, which is called inflation targeting. This strategy has three characteristics: (i) an announced numerical inflation target, (ii) monetary policy decisions are primarily based on differences between inflation forecasts and this numerical target, and (iii) a high degree of transparency and accountability. Inflation targeting does not imply that the central bank only cares about price stability, in particular if flexible inflation targeting is pursued. Stabilization of the business cycle, i.e., fluctuations of economic activity around its trend, can be considered as well.

After the Global Financial Crisis in 2007/08, central bank mandates were reassessed. Adding a financial stability objective to the mandate was frequently considered (this is discussed more extensively in Chapter 3). In recent years, several major central banks engaged in a formal review of their monetary policy strategy. Chapter 2 explains what these reviews implied for the monetary policy strategy of the Federal Reserve, the European Central Bank and the Bank of England. It shows that these central banks have redesigned their strategy in a way that acknowledges that inflation that is too low can be as undesirable as inflation that is too high.

In the two decades leading up to the Global Financial Crisis, most central banks in advanced economies typically implemented monetary policy by steering short-term interest rates in the economy. This is generally referred to as conventional monetary policy. Simplifying: central banks raised or lowered money market rates through the use of their instruments if inflation and economic developments so required, i.e., raising interest rates if inflation became too high and lowering interest rates where the economic outlook deteriorated. However, there are limits as to how far the central bank can lower its policy rates to stimulate the economy. This is because the nominal short-term interest rate cannot be lowered (much) below zero, the so-called effective lower bound on interest rates. This lower bound reflects among others the fact that the public will prefer to keep funds in the form of cash rather than deposit them at a bank that charges negative rates on deposits (i.e., customers are charged to deposit their money). When policy rates are at their effective lower bound, central banks have other instruments at their disposal to stimulate the economy. These instruments are generally referred to as unconventional monetary policies. Probably the best-known are asset purchase programmes, often referred to as quantitative easing (QE). Under QE, the central bank purchases predetermined amounts of government bonds or other financial assets (such as corporate bonds). By buying financial assets in the open market from the private sector, the prices of those financial assets increase, thus lowering their yield.

As Chapter 2 explains, central banks can also use their communications as an instrument to shape market expectations. Central bank communication is the provision of information by the central bank to the public on the objectives of monetary policy, the monetary policy strategy, the economic outlook, and the outlook for future policy decisions. Central banks can use communication to influence financial market expectations about the future path of short-term interest rates, thereby affecting long-term interest rates. In addition, central bank communication may affect inflation expectations. Inflation expectations are important, as they will affect actual inflation. As Chapter 2 points out, one type of central bank communication that has become very popular is forward guidance, i.e., communicating about the future path of monetary policy.

Apart from monetary policy, several central banks nowadays also have a responsibility to maintain financial stability. Here a distinction can be made between micro- and macro-prudential supervision. Micro-prudential supervision aims to keep individual financial institutions safe in order to protect their customers. It does not focus on the financial system as a whole. In contrast, macro-prudential supervision aims to limit financial system-wide instability in order to protect the overall economy from significant economic welfare losses. This is important because even if all financial institutions look safe, there may still be serious risks to the financial system as a whole.

Chapter 3 focuses on central banks' role in maintaining financial stability. It first discusses the question of whether central banks should be responsible for micro-prudential supervision and then outlines micro-prudential supervision and the role of central banks therein. Next, it analyses macro-prudential policies. Finally, the chapter zooms in on crisis management. It is shown that, during the Global Financial Crisis of 2007/08 and the European sovereign debt crisis, central banks stepped in, even to such an extent that they were criticized for stretching or even overstepping their mandate. During the recent crisis induced by the COVID-19 pandemic, central banks intervened at an unprecedented scale.

The final chapter outlines five challenges faced by central banks. The first is low interest rates. At the time of writing, both short-term and long-term nominal interest have been low for an extended period of time. If policy rates are at their effective lower bound, central banks may have to resort to unconventional monetary policies, such as asset purchase programmes and forward guidance, to counter risks to price stability. There is a debate, both among academics and policy-makers, about the causes of these low interest rates. This discussion is generally framed in terms of the so-called natural interest rate, which is the real rate of interest consistent with full employment and stable prices. In the long run, the natural rate is determined by the supply of and demand for savings. The interest rate that equates supply and demand is the natural rate. Chapter 4 zooms in on what central banks can do to increase the natural rate, showing that two very different answers to that question have been put forward.

The second challenge is that central banks have imperfect knowledge about the underlying drivers of inflation and only control inflation imperfectly. Specifically, in the previous three decades monetary policy-makers have been confronted with several inflation puzzles. They were called puzzles because several potential explanations were suggested, all with different implications for future inflation and monetary policy. Interestingly, after a long period in which different factors have kept inflation relatively low, recently inflation increased in several advanced economies, exceeding the 2 per cent target that most central banks apply. Assessing what is the optimal monetary policy response depends on many different factors, including the persistence of shocks, how shocks transmit through the economy, how shocks impact the anchoring properties of inflation expectations, and how shocks impact the structural characteristics of the economy.

The third challenge is the coordination of monetary and fiscal policy, i.e., policies regarding government spending and taxes. In principle, both monetary and fiscal policy can be used to stabilize business cycles. A policy stance that tends to stabilize the business cycle is said to be countercyclical; otherwise, it is either neutral (i.e., no systematic impact on the cyclicality of economic activity) or procyclical (i.e., it tends to amplify fluctuations). An issue that is hotly debated in policy and academic circles alike is the proper mix of fiscal and monetary policy. The chapter shows that very frequently the coordination of monetary and fiscal policy is far from optimal.

Chapter 4 then summarizes the discussion about the reduced impact of monetary policy on inflation, looking at two dimensions of globalization, namely globalization of goods and labour markets, and financial globalization. As to the first, globalization is argued to have reduced inflation. For instance, the relocation of production to the most cost-efficient firms typically leads to a decline in the prices of goods that have been outsourced. Likewise, organizing production through so-called production chains, i.e., to produce the several components needed to produce a good at different places in the world (think mobile phones), makes those goods cheaper. As such goods' prices are a component of consumer prices, their fall contributed to low overall inflation. In addition to such direct effects, increased competition may also have indirect effects by moderating domestic producer prices.

Another explanation for the reduced scope for monetary policy to impact domestic inflation, is based on financial globalization. This can be explained using the so-called Mundell–Fleming Trilemma, according to which only two of the following three factors are compatible: exchange rate stability, open capital markets and domestic monetary autonomy. Under a fixed exchange rate regime, the scope for autonomous monetary policy is limited in the absence of capital restrictions. The reason is simple: If investors can move money from one country to another (open capital markets), and they believe that the price of one currency for another will remain constant over time (fixed exchange rates), then an equal interest rate in both countries is the only way to achieve currency market equilibrium. Thus, countries cannot simultaneously conduct their own monetary policy, maintain a fixed exchange rate and have free movement of capital. However, recent literature suggests that the monetary policy autonomy in a system of flexible exchange rates is also limited. In this view, even countries with flexible exchange rates do not have an independent monetary policy, as there is a global financial cycle, which is mainly determined by monetary policy in industrialized countries, in particular the US, and global risk aversion. Once the capital account is open, a global cycle would largely determine domestic financial conditions, i.e., the interest rates that non-financial corporates and households have to pay, irrespective of the ability of the domestic central bank to set the policy rate autonomously, and the prevailing exchange rate regime. In other words, the choice of the exchange rate regime is virtually irrelevant. There is no longer a trilemma (according to which only two of the three objectives, i.e., fixed exchange rate, autonomous monetary policy and free movement of capital, can be achieved simultaneously), but a dilemma: a choice between autonomous monetary policy or capital mobility.

Finally, Chapter 4 discusses climate change. There is overwhelming evidence that global temperatures are rising and that this is caused by human activities. In addition, there is increasing evidence that climate change and climate transition policies will have a profound impact on the financial system and the functioning of the economy. While governments are primarily responsible for taking climate action and setting climate policies, an increasing number of central banks started incorporating climate change considerations not only in their supervisory policies but also in their monetary policy frameworks, within their mandates.

NOTES

1. A monetary union consists of countries having a common currency and a common central bank. Probably the best know example is the euro area, which, at the time of writing consists of 19 European countries that have the euro as their currency. Within the euro area, the European Central Bank is responsible for monetary policy.
2. https://en.wikipedia.org/wiki/Central_bank.

1. Responsibilities and design of central banks

1.1 HISTORICAL BACKGROUND

During the twentieth century, central banking came of age. Figure 1.1 shows that there were only a few central banks at the start of the previous century. However, after the Second World War, when many countries that had formerly been colonies became independent, the number of central banks rapidly increased. The oldest existing central bank is the Sveriges Riksbank, the central bank of Sweden, which was created in 1668. The origination of central banks differs. This section discusses the history of the Bank of England, the US Federal Reserve System (the Fed) and the European Central Bank, illustrating their different backgrounds.

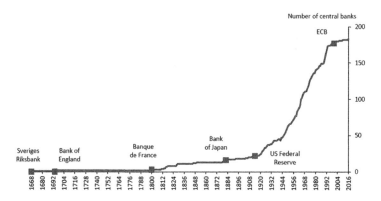

Figure 1.1   Number of central banks

Note: The figure shows the number of central banks in the world.
Source: Haldane (2017).

1.1.1   The Bank of England

Like most other central banks, the Bank of England (BoE) was created by government (Goodhart, 2018). It was founded in 1694, but not as a central bank. In fact, the concept of a central bank did not exist in the seventeenth century and only came into use in the late nineteenth century (Bordo and Siklos, 2018).[1] The BoE was established as a private joint stock, limited liability company in order to finance an, at the time, ongoing war with France. The bank was given certain special advantages: it was, for instance, the only joint stock bank then allowed in England. The government used the BoE, with the bank managing the government's cash flows and advising on debt management. Its privileged position made the BoE the dominant commercial bank in London. Other London banks held deposits with the BoE, which facilitated payments. Rather than transport gold specie, at great cost and some risk, any depositor at the BoE could arrange for a payment to be made by drawing on its deposit at the BoE. Furthermore, almost all other London banks ceased issuing their own banknotes, although banks outside London continued to issue their notes.

The Bank of England is generally viewed as the first central bank to successfully become a lender of last resort (LoLR) for banks. This means that the central bank, if needed, can assist banks in converting their non-cash assets into cash, or by providing financial assistance (see Calomiris *et al.*, 2016 for further details).

Despite its unique status, for a very long time, the BoE competed with other banks. In fact, only from 1914 onwards, it effectively ceased its activities as a commercial bank (Goodhart, 2018). In 1946, the BoE was nationalized, although this was a purely symbolic gesture.[2] The relationship with the government remained exactly as before, with the BoE subservient to the government in respect of all key decisions (Goodhart, 2018). In 1997, the BoE became operationally independent of the government in line with many other central banks (see section 1.3).

During the greater part of the BoE's existence, its main policy objective was to maintain an external standard (Goodhart, 2018). For most years until 1931, this was maintenance of the Gold Standard, while after the Second World War it was to hold the exchange rate pegged against the US dollar under the Bretton Woods system (see Box 1.1). The BoE was certainly not unique in this regard. Most central banks were in a similar position until the Bretton Woods system collapsed in the 1970s. In essence, policies by central banks under these regimes were as follows: central banks raised interest rates to protect the peg when foreign exchange reserves were falling, and lowered interest rates when the reverse was happening (Goodhart, 2018).

BOX 1.1 THE GOLD STANDARD AND THE BRETTON WOODS SYSTEM[3]

Under the Gold Standard, participating countries fixed the prices of their domestic currencies in terms of a specified amount of gold. National money was freely convertible into a fixed amount of gold. The period from 1880 to 1914 is known as the classical Gold Standard. During that time, the majority of countries adhered (in varying degrees) to gold.

The system was supposed to work as follows. A country with a balance-of-payment surplus would see an inflow of gold, which would raise prices and economic activity in that country. This, in turn, would bring about an increase in imports, thereby reducing the balance-of-payments surplus. The gold in-flows would continue until balances of payments would be in equilibrium again. If a country had a balance-of-payments deficit, this mechanism would work in the opposite direction, i.e., the outflow of gold would reduce prices and economic activity in that country, which would bring about a decrease in imports from other countries. To stimulate these gold flows, central banks were supposed to raise their discount rates—the interest rate at which the central bank lends money to other banks—to speed a gold inflow, and to lower their discount rates to facilitate a gold outflow.

As countries maintained a fixed price for gold, exchange rates were fixed. And because exchange rates were fixed, price levels around the world moved together. Against the backdrop of the Great Depression starting in 1929, most countries abandoned the Gold Standard in the 1930s.

Between 1946 and 1971, the Bretton Woods system was in place. Under this system, all participating national currencies were valued in relation to the US dollar, which became the dominant reserve currency. Countries had a fixed exchange rate against the dollar. Currencies were only allowed to deviate from these rates within a band of plus and minus 1 per cent. The dollar, in turn, was convertible to gold at the fixed rate of $35 per ounce. Due to persistent balance-of-payments deficits, the US gold reserves declined, reducing confidence in the ability of the US to redeem its currency in gold. On 15 August 1971, President Nixon announced that the US would no longer redeem currency for gold.

Under the 1971 Smithsonian Agreement, the major countries in the world agreed to raise the price of gold to $38 per ounce. Other countries revalued their currency by up to 10 per cent. The band for exchange rate fluctuations was increased to 2.25 per cent from 1 per cent. But the Smithsonian agreement also proved to be ineffective, and the Bretton Woods system collapsed in 1973.

1.1.2   The Federal Reserve System

After two failed attempts to establish a central bank, the Federal Reserve System was created in 1913. Eichengreen (2018) attributes the failure of the two previous attempts to a strong popular opposition to a single powerful financial institution. This led to the refusal of the US Congress (by a single vote) to renew the charter of the First Bank of the United States (1791–1811) and to President Andrew Jackson's veto of the bill to renew the charter of the Second Bank of the United States (1816–1836) in 1832. In the intermediate period, known as the Free Banking Era, the US had no central bank and US banking was a hodgepodge of state-chartered banks. These banks issued their own paper notes and were not subject to federal regulation. As pointed out by Bernanke (2015a), the absence of a central bank had serious drawbacks. Most obviously, the country had no public institution that could respond to the recurring bank runs and financial panics that buffeted the economy, including major panics in 1837, 1857, 1873, 1893 and 1907.

The Federal Reserve Act was signed into law on 23 December 1913 by President Woodrow Wilson. The law provided for a maximum of 12 regional Reserve Banks, each with a governor and a board of directors.[4] The law also established the Federal Reserve Board in Washington DC. The 1913 Federal Reserve Act did not specify the governance relationship between and among the Federal Reserve Board and the Reserve Banks. In fact, each of the 12 Reserve Banks could decide on its discount rates, i.e., the interest rate that commercial banks and other depository institutions pay when they borrow from a Reserve Bank. As a consequence, between 1913 and 1935 (a period called "decades of disaster" by

Eichengreen, 2018), there were constant struggles between the regional Reserve Banks and the Board in Washington. It was with the adoption of the Glass–Steagall Act by Congress in 1933—in response to a national banking crisis—that the Federal Open Market Committee was established as the formal central decision-making body responsible for open market operations (one of the main instruments of monetary policy that will be explained in more detail in section 2.3) of the regional Reserve Banks.

The governance of the Fed as we know it today has much of its origin in the Banking Act of 1935 and its amendment in 1942. The Fed received a monopoly to issue banknotes. Until then, both private-issued and government-issued banknotes were simultaneously in circulation, while before 1914 private banks issued banknotes. The Act led to a system that represented a much more centralized system than every previous central bank design in US history. Most importantly, it created the Board of Governors of the Federal Reserve System. Heads of the Federal Reserve Banks would no longer carry the name "governor" but would be "president". The title of governor would be reserved for the members of the Board of Governors. The Federal Open Market Committee (FOMC), which takes decisions about monetary policy, was also reformed. Nowadays, it consists of twelve members: the seven members of the Board of Governors; the president of the Federal Reserve Bank of New York; and four of the remaining eleven Reserve Bank presidents, who serve one-year terms on a rotating basis.[5] Non-voting Reserve Bank presidents attend FOMC meetings and participate in discussions. The 1935 Banking Act also booted representatives of the President's administration from the Board of Governors (Conti-Brown, 2015).

As in the past, the private sector is still involved in the Federal Reserve System. Commercial banks that are members of the Federal Reserve System hold stock in their District's Reserve Bank and elect six of the Reserve Bank's directors; the three remaining directors are appointed by the Board of Governors. Presidents must be approved by the Board of Governors for five-year terms.

1.1.3   The European Central Bank

Different from the BoE and the Fed, the European Central Bank (ECB) is of much younger age, having been founded in 1998. Furthermore, unlike the BoE and the Fed, which only serve the UK and the US, respectively, the ECB is the central bank for several European countries that have adopted the euro as its single currency. At the time of writing, the euro is the official currency of 19 European Union (EU) Member States (but this number will increase as explained in Box 1.2) with around 340 million citizens.[6]

After the Second World War, several European countries strived for economic integration, culminating in what is known today as the EU.[7] A major step in the history of European integration was the publication of the report of the Committee for the Study of Economic and Monetary Union in 1989. The Delors Report—named after the chairman of this committee and then-president of the European Commission[8] Jacques Delors—proposed a three-phase transition towards monetary unification, i.e., a common currency and a common monetary policy for all participating EU Member States. Its main conclusions were incorporated into the 1992 Maastricht Treaty, which formed the basis for European monetary unification (see Box 1.2). The Economic and Monetary Union (EMU) was launched on 1 January 1999 with the irrevocable fixing of the exchange rates of the then 11 participating countries and the introduction of the euro. The ECB became responsible for monetary policy in the euro area—the third-largest economic area in the world after China and the United States. In January 2002, physical euro banknotes and coins were brought into circulation.

Before EMU, European countries had their own currencies. After the breakdown of Bretton Woods, several countries made different attempts to stabilize their bilateral exchange rates, most recently before the introduction of the euro by participating in the Exchange Rate Mechanism (ERM). Currencies participating in the ERM were supposed to fluctuate vis-à-vis one another within a band of plus or minus 2.25 per cent around agreed-upon central rates that could be adjusted. Although this system brought some stability to the participating currencies, it only had mixed success. At times, there were frequent adjustments of the central rates. In 1992–1993, the currencies of several participating countries plummeted vis-à-vis the German D-mark. A common currency would take this exchange rate instability away. At the same time, critics noted that the absence of potential exchange rate adjustments could come at the cost of introducing instability elsewhere within the system.

Within the ERM system, the German D-Mark functioned as the anchor. Countries that pegged their currency to Germany's had little room for manoeuvre in monetary policy-making. If the German monetary authorities decided to change their interest rates in response to the domestic economic situation, the other countries had to follow if they wanted to maintain their peg. Various countries, notably France, therefore felt that the German-dominated ERM did not always serve their interests. A monetary union was often regarded as the solution to this problem.

A third impetus for monetary unification came from economic integration. The EU strived to create an internal market by 1992. It was believed that, in order to reap the full gains from the internal market, exchange rate risks and transaction costs—converting currencies is costly—were to be banished by introducing a common currency. Although there is no consensus among economists on the view that fixed exchange rates are needed to fully capture the gains from the single market, the argument gained popularity among policy-makers.

In EMU, decisions about monetary policy in the euro area are taken by the ECB's Governing Council, which consists of the six members of the ECB Executive Board and the governors of the national central banks of the countries in the euro area (nineteen as of 2019). The latter are appointed by their respective governments. The Executive Board of the ECB consists of the president, vice-president and four other members. Its members are appointed by the European Council.[9] Executive Board members serve a non-renewable, eight-year term in office. As the ECB is an institution of the European Union servicing European citizens, when taking monetary policy decisions, the members of the Governing Council focus on the euro area as a whole and not on their own country.

BOX 1.2 BECOMING PART OF THE EURO AREA

At the time of writing, the euro area consists of 19 out of 27 EU Member States. Yet, all remaining Member States except Denmark are required to adopt the euro at some point in the future. To achieve this, they must satisfy specific criteria known as "convergence criteria", also known as the Maastricht Criteria, named after the city in the Netherlands in which the European Treaty that established the Economic and Monetary Union was signed. These criteria relate to inflation, long-term interest rates, exchange rate stability, and public deficit and debt-to-GDP ratios (see Table 1.1). The EU countries that have expressed the clearest intention to adopt the euro in the near term are Croatia and Bulgaria. In June 2021, the Prime Minister of Croatia announced that the country's goal is to join the euro area on 1 January 2023. It is expected that Bulgaria intends to join one year later. As this is one of the convergence criteria to affirm exchange rate stability, Bulgaria and Croatia joined the ERM II mechanism in July 2020. At that time, they also joined the Banking Union (see section 3.2) so that their significant banking institutions came under the direct supervision of the ECB. In June 2022, euro area Finance Ministers issued a recommendation that Croatia would indeed become a member of the euro area as of 1 January 2023.

Whether it makes sense for a country to give up its own currency and monetary policy for the euro and the monetary policy of the ECB critically depends on how similar the economic situation in that country is to that in the euro area. The more similar the business cycles of the countries that intend to join the euro area, the more likely it will be that the ECB's monetary policy—which focuses on the inflation outlook for the euro area as a whole—will benefit them. If inflation and the business cycle in Bulgaria and Croatia differ from inflation and the business cycle in the euro area, these countries will not get the monetary policy that would fit with their economic situation. However, research has shown that joining the monetary union will increase business cycle coherence. Introducing a common currency will increase trade, and more trade will increase business cycle coherence of the countries in the monetary union (see de Haan *et al.* (2008) for a further discussion of this literature).

1.1.4   Conclusions

Although the central banks of the UK, the US and the euro area have a very different historical background, there is one commonality, namely that political interests and the economic problems at the time played a key role in the gestation and the design of central banks. This is not unique to these central banks. Often a fiscal motivation (e.g., war finance) or an attempt to stem the incidence of financial crises can explain the creation of a central bank (Bordo and Siklos, 2018).

Table 1.1   Convergence criteria

Inflation	Member State has a price performance that is sustainable and an average rate of inflation, observed over a period of one year before the examination, that does not exceed by more than 1.5 percentage points that of, at most, the three best-performing Member States in terms of price stability.
Interest rate	Member State has had an average nominal long-term interest rate that does not exceed by more than 2 percentage points that of, at most, the three best-performing Member States in terms of price stability.
Exchange rate	Member State has observed the normal fluctuation margins provided for by the ERM II* for at least two years, without devaluing against the currency of any other Member State on its own initiative.
Budget deficit	Member State's planned or actual government deficit to GDP ratio must not exceed 3 per cent unless: – either the ratio has declined substantially and continuously and reached a level that comes close to the reference value; or – the excess over the reference value is only exceptional and temporary and the ratio remains close to the reference value.
Debt	Member State's government debt-to-GDP ratio must not exceed 60 per cent, unless the ratio is sufficiently diminishing and approaching the reference value at a satisfactory pace.

*ERM II is the successor of the ERM after the introduction of the euro, which aims to stabilise the exchange rates of participating countries vis-à-vis the euro.

1.2   MANDATES OF CENTRAL BANKS

As became clear from the description of their historical roles in section 1.1, central banks have several responsibilities, including issuing banknotes and acting as "lender of last resort" for financial institutions. Nowadays, the most important responsibility of central banks is monetary policy. This section discusses the objectives of monetary policy.

In the last decades, the general consensus has been that central banks should aim for a low but positive inflation rate (section 2.1 discusses this in more detail). For instance, on its website, the Bank of England (BoE) states: "We are responsible for keeping inflation (price rises) low and stable. The Government has set us a target of keeping inflation at 2%."[10]

Moreover, "[l]ow and stable inflation is good for the UK's economy and it is our main monetary policy aim. We also support the Government's other economic aims for growth and employment. Sometimes, in the short term, we need to balance our target of low inflation with supporting economic growth and jobs."[11] Similarly, the Bank of Japan Act states that the Bank's monetary policy should be "aimed at achieving price stability, thereby contributing to the sound development of the national economy."[12]

Like the BoE and the Bank of Japan, the ECB aims at stable prices. The Maastricht Treaty made price stability the ECB's primary objective, but left it to the ECB to define this objective. Over time, the ECB has reassessed how its primary mandate of price stability is best maintained, most recently after the review of its monetary policy strategy that was concluded in July 2021 (see section 2.2). In addition to having price stability as its primary mandate, the Treaty stipulates: "without prejudice to the objective of price stability", the ECB "shall support the general economic policies in the Union with a view to contributing to the achievement of the objectives of the Union." These latter objectives include balanced economic growth, a highly competitive social market economy aiming at full employment and social progress, and a high level of protection and improvement of the quality of the environment.

Not all central banks have a singular primary objective. For instance, the Federal Reserve's mandate is "to promote effectively the goals of maximum employment, stable prices, and moderate long-term interest rates." As long-term interest rates can remain low only in a stable macroeconomic environment, these goals are often referred to as the dual mandate—maximum employment and price stability. Figure 1.2 shows that the Fed is not unique in this regard. The figure shows the extent to which 126 central banks around the world (other than those in the US, the euro area, Japan and the UK) strive for price stability. All central banks receive a score between zero (no importance) and one, depending on the importance of price stability as their objective.[13] Almost all central banks have a reference to price stability in their mandate with most of those central banks having a clear priority for price stability (92 central banks having a score of 0.6 or higher). At the same time, there are 30 central banks that have objectives other than price stability, which may at times conflict with price stability (i.e., a score of 0.4).

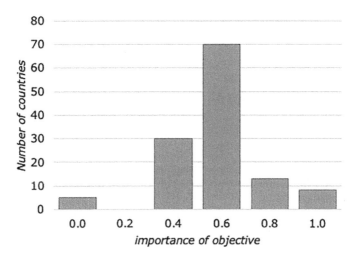

Figure 1.2   Importance of price stability in the mandates of central banks

Note: The figure shows the frequency distribution of the importance of price stability in the mandate of 126 central banks in 2015 using the scores shown in endnote 13.
Source: Updates of Bodea and Hicks (2015).

Apart from monetary policy, several central banks also have a responsibility for maintaining financial stability. Here a distinction can be made between micro- and macro-prudential supervision. Micro-prudential supervision aims to limit the distress of individual financial institutions, with the ultimate objective of protecting their customers. It does not focus on the financial system as a whole. In contrast, macro-prudential supervision aims to limit financial system-wide distress, with the ultimate objective of protecting the overall economy from significant losses in economic welfare. This is important because, even if all financial institutions look safe, there may still be serious risks to the financial system as a whole. For instance, if many banks have common exposures (say, exposures on a local real estate market), a shock (say, an increase in local unemployment) may affect all these banks at the same time. After the Global Financial Crisis, macro-prudential policy became much more advanced with the development of specific policy tools and the formal allocation of policy responsibilities. The financial stability objective of central banks will be discussed in Chapter 3. That chapter will also explain how micro- and macro-prudential supervision is organized in some of the main advanced economy central banks.

1.3   INSTITUTIONAL DESIGN OF CENTRAL BANKS

1.3.1   Decision-making by committees

After the Second World War, most central banks were dominated by a single decision-maker. Central banks were seen as top-down institutions with extraordinary authority vested in the governor. Nowadays, most central banks are run by committees, like the BoE's Monetary Policy Committee (MPC), the Bank of Japan's Policy Board, the Fed's FOMC and the ECB's Governing Council. As pointed out by Blinder (2007), one of the reasons for this trend is the spread of central bank independence (see section 1.3.3). As Blinder (2007: 107) puts it: "When the central bank was just following orders communicated by the government, there was not much reason to have a committee on the other end of the phone. An individual governor sufficed—and also limited the phone bill."

As pointed out by Blinder (2007), decision-making by a committee has several advantages. First, it provides some insurance against the possibly extreme preferences of an individual central banker, for example, a person who might be obsessed with either low inflation or low unemployment.[14] Second, pooling knowledge in an uncertain world should lead to better analysis and forecasts, and, therefore, to better decisions. Third, a group of diverse people who process information and reach decisions differently may outperform even highly skilled individuals when it comes to the execution of complex tasks.

1.3.2   Centralization vs. Decentralization

As became clear from section 1.1, the extent to which decision-making about monetary policy is centralized or decentralized is important, notably in large currency unions. There are major differences in this respect across the major central banks. Compared with other major central banks, the ECB's Governing Council is large and contains a higher proportion of voting outsiders (see Table 1.2). By contrast, for example,

Table 1.2   Main characteristics of selected monetary policy
committees

Country	MPC size	Number of "outsiders"	De jure decision rule	Non-voting MPC members
Euro area	25	19	Simple majority	4
United States	19	12	Simple majority	7
Japan	9	6	Simple majority	0
United Kingdom	9	4	Simple majority	0

Note: MPC is the Monetary Policy Committee, i.e., the body responsible for monetary policy decisions.
Source: de Haan *et al.* (2020).

seven of the twelve US Federal Reserve presidents do not vote as a result of the rotation system in place at the FOMC.

1.3.3   Central Bank Independence

Since the 1980s, the level of central bank independence (CBI) has increased considerably (see Figure 1.3).[15] Central bank independence refers to the absence of influence of politicians on monetary policy-making. The increase in CBI was based on the prevailing consensus among policy-makers and academics, that CBI leads to superior macroeconomic outcomes. As the former chair of the Board of Governors of the Federal Reserve System, Janet Yellen, puts it: "the ability of the central bank to make the decisions about monetary policy that it regards as in the best longer run interests of the economy free of short run political interference is very important", as "history shows, not only in the United States but around the world, that central bank independence promotes better economic performance."[16] The experience of Deutsche Bundesbank, the central bank of Germany, is often referred to in support of this view (see Box 1.3).

Economists consider delegating monetary policy to an independent central bank that has a clear mandate to strive for price stability as a commitment device. With an independent and inflation-averse central bank in charge of monetary policy, the upward inflation bias due to the so-called

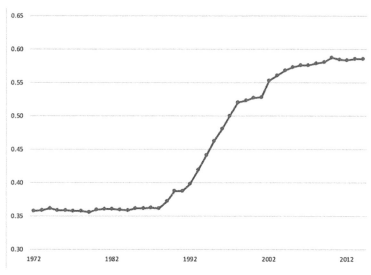

Figure 1.3   Average central bank independence in the world,
1970–2014

Note: The figure shows the world average of the CBI index of Cukierman *et al.*
(1992).
Source: Updates of Bodea and Hicks (2015).

time-inconsistency problem is much less than when the government is in charge of monetary policy (Rogoff, 1985). This time-inconsistency problem arises due to the short-term benefits that surprise inflation can have, such as lowering unemployment and reducing the real value of government debt. The government may be tempted to reap the short-term benefits of surprise inflation even if the long-term costs of such a policy may be high. In the words of another former Fed Chair Ben Bernanke (2010), "a central bank subject to short-term political influences would likely not be credible when it promised low inflation, as the public would recognize the risk that monetary policy-makers could be pressured to pursue short-run expansionary policies that would be inconsistent with long-run price stability. When the central bank is not credible, the public will expect high inflation and, accordingly, demand more-rapid increases in nominal wages and in prices. Thus, lack of independence of the central bank can lead to higher inflation and inflation expectations in the longer run, with no offsetting benefits in terms of greater output or employment."

BOX 1.3   THE BANK "THAT RULED EUROPE"

During the last decades of the previous century, the Deutsche Bundesbank (Bundesbank for short) was considered a very powerful public sector institution. Marsh (1992) even described the German central bank as "the bank that rules Europe", reflecting *inter alia* the anchor role of the German D-mark in the ERM as discussed in section 1.1.3. The historical experience of the Bundesbank also informed the debate in Europe on the design choices for monetary institutions in the last decades of the twentieth century (Issing, 2008). In short, the Bundesbank was considered very independent (reflecting a strong anti-inflation sentiment among the German population), while Germany's inflation performance was at the time better than that of most other advanced economies. However, this popular view needs some nuance. Most importantly, the independence of the German central bank was imposed by the western Allied forces (notably the US) after the Second World War and certainly did not reflect preferences of German politicians at the time. In fact, on more than one occasion did German politicians try to limit the Bundesbank's externally imposed independence. As the Bundesbank was able to muster public support for its independence, these attempts failed (see de Haan, 2018 for a more detailed account).

The time-inconsistency problem of monetary policy can be reduced if monetary authority is delegated to a central bank that has both instrument-independence and is conservative. Instrument-independence means that government influence on monetary policy-making is limited. Conservative here means that the central bank is more averse to deviations of inflation from target than the government. If the central bank were to have the same preferences as the government, it would follow the same policies as the government and independence would not matter. Likewise, if the central bank were fully under the spell of the government, its inflation aversion would not matter. Only if the central bank is more inflation-averse than the government, and able to decide on monetary policy without political interference, can it credibly promise to keep inflation in line with its target.

The empirical prediction that follows from this theory, namely that countries with an independent and conservative central bank will have lower inflation than those in which monetary policy is controlled by the government, has been tested extensively. In their meta regression analysis of these empirical studies, Klomp and de Haan (2010: 612) conclude that their evidence "corroborates the conventional view by finding a significant ... effect of CBI on inflation."

Although there is thus a strong case for instrument-independence, i.e., the ability of the central bank to decide on the use of its instruments without political interference, this is different for goal-independence, i.e., the ability of the central bank to set its own goals for monetary policy. The argument against goal-independence is that, in a democracy, the government is accountable to the electorate and their representatives in parliament. As central bankers are not elected, the ultimate goals of monetary policy should therefore be set by the elected government. Indeed, it seems that a "broad consensus has emerged among policymakers, academics, and other informed observers around the world that the goals of monetary policy should be established by the political authorities, but that the conduct of monetary policy in pursuit of those goals should be free from political control" (Bernanke, 2010). Central banks, in other words, have a delegated authority to achieve their legally mandated objective(s) and should have instrument-independence to reach their objective(s). Still, politicians frequently try to influence central bank policies as discussed in Box 1.4.

BOX 1.4 THE END OF CENTRAL BANK INDEPENDENCE?

President Recep Tayyip Erdoğan of Turkey has dismissed three central bank governors within 20 months between July 2019 and March 2021. Each time, he made it plain that he did so for their failure to follow his wishes over monetary policy.[17] Political interference with monetary policy is not confined to emerging market economies. In one of his tweets, former US president Trump stated: "The Fed Rate, over a fairly short period of time, should be reduced by at least 100 basis points, with perhaps some quantitative easing as well. If that happened, our Economy would be even better, and the World Economy would be greatly and quickly enhanced – good for everyone!"

Are these examples business as usual or are the heydays of CBI over? There are some reasons why CBI should not be taken for granted. First, it seems that many have excessive and unrealistic expectations about what central banks can achieve. As the Bank for International Settlement's Annual Report (BIS, 2016: 22) puts it: "the extraordinary burden placed on central banking since the crisis is generating growing strains. During the Great Moderation,[18] markets and the public at large came to see central banks as all-powerful. Post-crisis, they have come to expect the central bank to manage the economy, restore full employment, ensure strong growth, preserve price stability and foolproof the financial system. But in fact, this is a tall order on which the central bank alone cannot deliver. The extraordinary measures taken to stimulate the global economy have sometimes tested the boundaries of the institutions. As a consequence, risks to its reputation, perceived legitimacy and independence have been rising."

Another threat to independence lies in central bank policies. After the crisis, central banks in advanced economies introduced unconventional monetary policies (such as asset purchase programmes, discussed in more detail in section 2.3). Furthermore, as noted above, many of them introduced macro-prudential policies. These new policies may have stronger distributional implications than conventional monetary policies (Colciago et al., 2019). Of course, decisions by central banks will always affect relative prices and therefore their decisions will have redistributive effects, but over the cycle these effects more or less balance out. However, macro-prudential and unconventional monetary policies may have much stronger distributional consequences than conventional monetary policies, and this has potential implications for the central bank's independence.[19] It is widely believed that policies that have strong and permanent distributional consequences should not be left to unelected technocrats.

Has CBI been reduced since the Global Financial Crisis? de Haan et al. (2018) compare the average level of legal CBI before, during and after the start of the financial crisis for several groups of countries. Their evidence does not suggest that CBI has decreased after the crisis. However, politicians seeking to influence monetary policy, while not changing central bank legislation, may use other means to undermine CBI, for instance, by filling important positions at central banks with individuals that they believe are favourably predisposed towards their preferred policies. de Haan et al. (2018) therefore also present average turnover rates of central bank governors for different groups of countries before and after the crisis. Their results do not suggest that the number of central bank governor turnovers has changed since the crisis in most country groups. However, in the group of advanced economies the turnover rate increased somewhat, which suggests that in some countries there may have been an increase in political pressure on central banks.

Another way of enhancing credibility is to delegate monetary authority to an independent and conservative (i.e., inflation-averse) foreign central bank by fixing the exchange rate. A high inflation problem is one important motivation for small, open economies to consider introducing a credible exchange rate peg. However, before a country decides in favour of such a regime, a proper comparison with the alternative of an independent and inflation-averse central bank should be made. Both alternatives have advantages and disadvantages, and it is not always obvious what the optimum solution would be. Two considerations affect this choice. First, a fixed exchange rate regime becomes more attractive when the home (foreign) country's central bank is relatively dependent (independent) and output oriented (inflation oriented). Second, a fixed exchange rate regime is more attractive the more the economic developments in the home country are similar to those in the foreign country. Behind this is the simple fact that the more similar both countries are, the more likely that foreign monetary policy is in line with the needs of the home economy.[20]

1.4   TRANSPARENCY AND ACCOUNTABILITY OF CENTRAL BANKS

Former Fed Chairman Ben Bernanke (2013) writes: "when I began my time as Chairman, one of my priorities was to make ... monetary policy as transparent and open as reasonably possible. ... [T]ransparency in monetary policy enhances public understanding and confidence, promotes informed discussion of policy options, increases the accountability of monetary policymakers for reaching their mandated objectives, and ultimately makes policy more effective by tightening the linkage between monetary policy, financial conditions, and the real economy."[21]

Figure 1.4 illustrates how central bank transparency has evolved. As Figure 1.4 shows, central bank transparency has increased remarkably.[22] Apparently, Bernanke was not the only central banker who thinks that transparency is important. The strongest increase is visible in high-income countries, but central banks in less advanced economies have become more transparent as well.

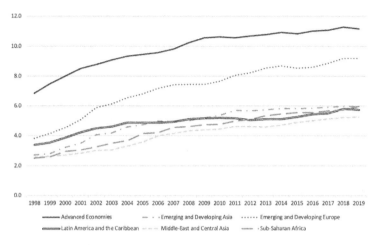

Figure 1.4   Central bank transparency

Note: The figure shows the central bank transparency index of Eijffinger and Geraats (2006) for several groups of countries.
Source: Dincer and Eichengreen (2014).

Dincer and Eichengreen (2014) pose that central bank transparency is a means to enhance the credibility of the central bank. A commitment to maintain low and stable inflation will be more convincing when the central bank explains in detail how and why its policies are supposed to deliver on this objective. In turn, a more credible commitment gives the central bank more leeway to deviate from normal policies when atypical conditions arise, since it would be clear to the public that this deviation would be temporary and not inconsistent with the longer-term objective of monetary policy.

As is apparent from the quote from Bernanke, central bank transparency is considered a crucial element of central bank accountability. It is widely believed that more independent central banks should be accountable. In a principal–agent approach, the essence of accountability is that once a principal (such as the legislator) delegates a particular task to an agent (the central bank, in this example) and gives the agent instruments to perform this task, the agent must be held accountable for achieving the objective. This means that the principal must form an opinion of the agent's performance. In other words, a central bank should be required to regularly report on its past performance and future plans. There are various possibilities for this, ranging from reports, minutes, testimony to legislatures and other communication devices (see Blinder *et al.*, 2008 for an extensive discussion).

Despite the widespread support for the notion of central bank accountability, there is not a consensus in the literature about its precise definition. de Haan *et al.* (2005) argue that the concept of central bank accountability has three main features: (1) decisions about the explicit definition and ranking of the objectives of monetary policy; (2) disclosure of actual monetary policy; and (3) clarity on who bears final responsibility with respect to monetary policy.

In practice, in most advanced economies elected politicians decide on the explicit definition and ranking of objectives of monetary policy. This ensures that there is adequate democratic legitimacy for the objectives that monetary policy pursues, which is particularly important when central banks are subject to a large degree of instrument-independence.

Transparency is a very important element of accountability as well. Where the reasoning behind and strength of opinion supporting certain monetary policy decisions are clear, it is easier to make a judgment and to hold central bank officials accountable for their behaviour. So, a central bank should be required to report in regular intervals on its past performance and future plans. For instance, central banks should explain how they respond to a deviation of forecasts and/or outcomes from the objectives of monetary policy, i.e., they should explain their reaction function.

With respect to the final responsibility for monetary policy, de Haan *et al.* (2005) pose that three issues are crucial: the relationship with parliament, the existence of some kind of override mechanism and the dismissal procedure for the central bank governor. In their view, parliaments have to play a major role in the democratic accountability of central banks.

Parliaments should have the opportunity to review central banks' performance with regard to monetary policy on a regular basis, while central banks at the same time can explain and justify their conduct. In general, parliaments always hold the ultimate responsibility for monetary policy since they can change the legal basis of the central bank. Indeed, the mere threat of a change of the law may ensure that even highly legally independent central banks will ensure that monetary policy will be broadly in accordance with the wishes of elected politicians. To ensure that this does not encroach on the independence of central banks, central bank mandates can be codified in legislation that require more than a single, simple majority to be amended.

The central bank may not (only) be directly accountable to parliament but (also) to the government, which, in turn, is accountable to parliament. In that case, it is important that the government is able to influence central bank behaviour. If the government does not interfere, it apparently agrees with central bank policies and can be held accountable for this by parliament. Such a mechanism existed in the Netherlands before the change of the Dutch central bank law when the Netherlands adopted the euro. However, if such an override mechanism exists, it is crucial that the conditions under which it can be applied are laid down in detail. It has to be ensured that the mechanism is not used as a tool for undesired political influence. The procedure for the application for the override mechanism itself needs to be transparent. The decision to apply the override mechanism should be made public. Furthermore, the procedure to apply an override should provide for some kind of review (like a possibility for the central bank to appeal) to make sure that the override is being used carefully.

Finally, the dismissal procedure for a central banker can be a mechanism of ex post accountability if a central bank official can be dismissed on grounds of bad performance, that is, not realizing stated objectives. Obviously, a central banker should not be dismissed because the government does not agree with policy decisions taken.

NOTES

1. In the nineteenth and the beginning of the twentieth century, several central banks were created (Bordo and Siklos, 2018). The banks founded included the Banque de France (1800), De Nederlandsche Bank (1814), the Norges Bank (1816), the First and Second Banks of the United States (1791 and 1816), the Reichsbank (1873), the Bank of Japan (1882), the Banca d'Italia (1893), the Swiss National Bank (1907) and the US Federal Reserve (1913).
2. Nowadays, most central banks are government owned, although there are exceptions, such as the Swiss central bank.
3. This part heavily draws on Michael Bordo's description of the Gold Standard, which is available here: https://www.econlib.org/library/Enc/GoldStandard .html
4. The US has been divided into 12 Federal Reserve Districts, with Banks in Boston, New York, Philadelphia, Cleveland, Richmond, Atlanta, Chicago, St. Louis, Minneapolis, Kansas City, Dallas and San Francisco.
5. The rotating seats are filled from the following four groups of Banks, one Bank president from each group: Boston, Philadelphia and Richmond; Cleveland and Chicago; Atlanta, St. Louis and Dallas; and Minneapolis, Kansas City and San Francisco.
6. The following EU Member States are part of the euro area: Austria, Belgium, Cyprus, Estonia, Finland, France, Germany, Greece, Ireland, Italy, Latvia, Lithuania, Luxembourg, Malta, the Netherlands, Portugal, Slovakia, Slovenia and Spain. Andorra, Monaco, San Marino and Vatican City have also adopted the euro as their national currency.
7. The next paragraphs heavily draw on de Haan *et al.* (2020).
8. The European Commission is the executive of the EU.
9. The European Council is made up of the heads of government or state and the president of the European Commission. Essentially, it defines the EU's policy agenda; it put forward major policy initiatives such as the Internal Market Programme, and the Maastricht Treaty.
10. At https://www.bankofengland.co.uk/monetary-policy/inflation
11. At https://www.bankofengland.co.uk/monetary-policy
12. At https://www.boj.or.jp/en/mopo/outline/index.htm/
13. The index is constructed as follows: Price stability mentioned as the major or only objective in the charter, and in case of conflict with government central bank has final authority to pursue policies aimed at achieving this goal = 1.0; Price stability is the only objective = 0.8; Price stability is only one goal, with other compatible objectives = 0.6; Price stability is only one goal, with potentially conflicting objectives, such as full employment = 0.4; No objectives stated in the bank charter = 0.2; Stated objectives do not include price stability = 0.0.
14. Central bankers may have different preferences: some (the "hawks") may be far more concerned with inflation, while others (the "doves") put more weight on unemployment. The clearer the mandate of the central bank, the less these personal preferences should matter. As Blinder (2007: 108) points out, if the central bank's legal mandate is less precise, such as the Federal

Reserve's mandate "to pursue both 'stable prices' and 'maximum employment,' committee members have much more scope for interpreting their mandate differently. And they do."

15. The figure shows updates of the Cukierman et al. (1992) index provided by Bodea and Hicks (2015). This index is based on four characteristics of the central bank's charter. First, a bank is viewed as more independent if the governor is appointed by the central bank board rather than by the government, is not subject to dismissal, and has a long term of office. Second, the level of independence is higher the greater the extent to which policy decisions are made without government involvement. Third, a central bank is more independent if its charter states that price stability is the sole or primary goal of monetary policy. Fourth, independence is greater if there are limitations on the government's ability to borrow from the central bank.

16. Source: https://www.reuters.com/article/us-usa-fed-highlights-idUSKBN0JV2 O320141217

17. See https://www.centralbanking.com/central-banks/governance/7902481/how -turkeys-president-created-chaos-in-economic-policy-making?utm_medium =email&_hsmi=190134528&_hsenc=p2ANqtz-9G53MnXmn4oIs1w9ipyK8Y nmaIv5QdBegiEWLiDnDGeLmwdgmC6nI5KHACDHdqxwdG1EVBal gQyLC5ThU66zNbj6s7OQ&utm_content=190134528&utm_source=hs_email

18. The Great Moderation is a period starting from the mid-1980s until 2007 characterized by low economic volatility and low inflation in advanced economies compared with the decades before. It ended with the Global Financial Crisis.

19. This is especially true for macro-prudential policies. Take, for instance, the case of a real estate boom that may turn into a bust. In the short run, the boom will increase the (apparent) wealth of homeowners and boost output in the construction business. Policy-makers could reduce the amplitude of both the boom and the bust by using macro-prudential policies, for instance by making caps on the loan-to-value (LTV) ratio more stringent. As these policies will hurt homeowners, the construction sector, and will make it more difficult for newcomers at the housing market to buy a house, such measures have redistributive consequences and are therefore politically not very attractive, especially if elections are near.

20. Apart from these considerations, several other advantages of fixed exchange rate regimes are mentioned in the literature that may be considered in deciding in favour or against a fixed exchange rate regime. First, fixed exchange rates reduce foreign currency risks in international trade and investment transactions. Second, fixed exchange rates can reduce the currency risk component in domestic interest rates. A fixed exchange rate regime also has drawbacks. First, the currency of the pegging country is susceptible to speculative attacks. Second, in emerging market countries an exchange rate peg can promote financial fragility and financial crisis, because often their debt is denominated in foreign currencies while financial assets are in domestic currency. Moreover, an exchange rate peg may encourage capital inflows, leading to a lending boom (Ghosh et al., 2014).

21. Bernanke (2013) argues that central bank transparency may enhance monetary policy effectiveness. In section 2.4 this view will be discussed more extensively.

22. The index shown has been developed by Eijffinger and Geraats (2006) and captures five dimensions of central bank transparency. *Political transparency* refers to openness about policy objectives, capturing the formal objectives of monetary policy, including an explicit prioritization in case of potentially conflicting goals, and quantitative targets. *Economic transparency* focuses on the economic information that is used for monetary policy. *Procedural transparency* is about the way monetary policy decisions are taken. *Policy transparency* means a prompt announcement of policy decisions. It also includes an explanation of the decision and a policy inclination or indication of likely future policy actions. *Operational transparency* concerns the implementation of the central bank's policy actions.

2. Monetary policy-making

2.1 FROM MONETARY TARGETING TO INFLATION TARGETING

2.1.1 Price stability as main objective

As explained in section 1.2, price stability is the primary (or even sole) objective of many central banks. Most central banks in advanced countries aim for *price stability*, which is generally defined as an inflation rate around 2 per cent over a specific policy horizon (see Table 2.1).

As highlighted by the Swedish central bank (the Riksbank), an inflation target "will function as a benchmark to guide expectations in the economy regarding future inflation. An inflation target makes it easier for households and companies to make well-founded economic decisions and lays the foundation for efficient price-setting and wage formation. The inflation target thus acts as the economy's 'nominal anchor'."[1] The Riksbank explains the virtues of price stability as follows: "High and fluctuating inflation leads to uncertainty over how prices will develop going forward, which means that interest rates and thereby borrowing costs will be higher than they would otherwise have been. It also becomes more difficult for households and companies to plan and to take financial decisions, and it affects the distribution of incomes and wealth between different groups in a random manner. All this can mean that willingness and ability to invest in new products and machinery declines and that activity in the economy as a whole is slowed down."

Most central banks define price stability as a stable and low, yet positive rate of inflation (i.e., as an inflation rate around two per cent). This does not square well with a literal interpretation of price stability implying that prices do not increase (i.e., an inflation rate of zero per cent). There are several reasons why central banks aim for a low rate of positive price increases in their pursuit of price stability (Blinder *et al.*, 2017). First, there may be upward biases in official estimates of inflation. This mismeasurement may result from several factors such as inadequate adjustments for improvement in the quality of goods and services and difficulties in incorporating new goods into the price index. Since the quality of goods typically increases over time, goods such as computers bought at two

Table 2.1   Price stability objective of some central banks

Country/ area	Objective	Definition
Canada	The inflation-control target is 2 per cent, the midpoint of a 1 to 3 per cent target range	Inflation measured using Consumer Price Index (CPI)
Euro area	The ECB considers that price stability is best maintained by aiming for 2 per cent inflation over the medium term	Year-on-year increase in the Harmonized Index for Consumer Prices (HICP) for the euro area
Japan	The Bank of Japan has set its price stability target at 2 per cent	Measured in terms of the year-on-year rate of change in CPI
UK	To keep inflation low and stable, the Government sets us an inflation target of 2 per cent	Inflation measured as 12-month increase in CPI
US	Inflation at the rate of 2 per cent is most consistent over the longer run with the Federal Reserve's statutory mandate*	Inflation measured by the annual change in the price index for personal consumption expenditures (PCE)
Sweden	The Riksbank's objective is to keep inflation around 2 per cent per year	Inflation measured as annual change in CPI with a fixed interest rate (CPIF)
Switzerland	Price stability is defined by the Swiss National Bank as a rise in the national consumer price index (CPI) of less than 2 per cent per annum	Inflation measured as annual change in CPI

*As explained in section 1.2, the Federal Reserve has a so-called dual mandate. Its objectives are, "to promote effectively the goals of maximum employment, stable prices and moderate long-term interest rates." The Fed announced a 2 per cent inflation target on 25 January 2012.
Source: Information taken from the central banks' websites.

different points in time are not directly comparable. Ignoring this quality change will induce a measurement error in the price index. Likewise, the prices of new goods often fall rapidly in the first years after their introduction. It may take several years before these new goods are included in the basket of goods used to calculate the price index, and thus the fall in their prices may be missed.

Second, a low rate of inflation may make it easier for firms to reduce real wages in the face of declining demand and non-flexible ("sticky") nominal wages. If inflation is close to zero, it will be difficult (or even impossible) for firms to lower workers' real wages if nominal wages are rigid. Firms may instead be forced to lay off workers, resulting in a higher unemployment rate. In contrast, with a low rate of inflation, firms can lower workers' real wages by keeping nominal wage increases below the rate of inflation so that unemployment does not rise.

Third, a low rate of inflation provides some insurance against deflation (a persistent decline in the general price level), which is generally regarded at least as serious a problem as high inflation. Buiter (2003) argues that deflation is not simply inflation with a negative sign, but it is rather a different regime that can change the functioning of the economy in several harmful ways. An important reason is that redistribution from debtors to creditors associated with deflation is more likely to lead to default and bankruptcy than redistributions from creditors to debtors associated with inflation. And these processes also destroy real resources. As a consequence, deflation may create a vicious cycle of rising real debt burdens and financial distress, which, in turn, may cause more downward pressure on prices. Likewise, persistent deflation may turn into a deflationary spiral of falling prices of goods. If firms and consumers expect prices to decline, they will postpone spending and thereby put further downward pressure on prices. According to Kuroda (2013), the governor of the Bank of Japan (BoJ), this is what happened during Japan's deflation since the latter half of the 1990: "behaviour based on recognition that 'prices would not rise' or 'prices would moderately decline' has been embedded in the economy."[2] Furthermore, if wages and prices are falling, borrowers' incomes may not increase enough to allow borrowers to keep up with their loan payments. This will force them to reduce other types of spending, and their weaker financial position will make it harder for them to obtain additional credit.

Finally, at very low levels of inflation, nominal interest rates will also be very low, limiting a central bank's ability to ease monetary policy in response to a weakening of the economic outlook. Once the policy rate reaches the effective lower bound, which may be below zero, conventional monetary easing becomes impossible (as will be explained in section 2.3).

Central banks may pursue different monetary policy strategies to meet their price stability objective. The next sections discuss some of these strategies.

2.1.2   Monetary targeting

In the past, several central banks had a *monetary targeting strategy*. This strategy was based on the monetarist presumption that inflation is always and everywhere a monetary phenomenon, or, in other words, that there is a tight link in the long run between inflation and the evolution of the supply of money circulating in the economy. If the money stock grows fast, the demand for goods increases. As the supply of goods in the short term will not increase to the same extent, prices of goods will go up. So, by keeping money growth in check, the central bank can maintain price stability.

The Deutsche Bundesbank, i.e., the central bank of Germany, is a prominent example of a central bank that had a monetary targeting strategy in the past. By aiming for a particular growth rate of the money stock (hence, monetary targeting), the bank strived for price stability. The Bundesbank's approach to derive money growth targets was based on the so-called *quantity equation of exchange*. This equation, which is most often associated with the American economist Irving Fisher, states that the quantity of money multiplied by the number of times that this money is spent in a given year, designated the velocity of money, must be equal to nominal income (the total nominal amount spent on goods and services in that year). This is an identity, i.e., a relationship that is true by definition. Irving Fisher reasoned that velocity is determined by the institutions in an economy that affect the way individuals conduct transactions. For instance, if people use credit cards to pay for their purchases, less money is required to conduct these transactions. As these institutions only slowly change, velocity can be considered as fairly constant in the short term. This implies that there is clear link between the money stock and nominal income.[3] Taking the sum of the (maximum) rise in prices the Bundesbank was willing to tolerate ("unavoidable inflation"), the predicted growth in potential output, and the expected trend rate of change in velocity gives the target for the desired change in the money stock (Deutsche Bundesbank, 1995).

The Bank of England also experimented with monetary targeting. As Goodhart (2018) explains, after the collapse of the Bretton Woods system in the early 1970s, the UK became a "pragmatic monetarist" with targets for a broad measure for the stock of money. While this policy led to falling inflation and a strong recovery from the deep recession of 1980–82, monetary targeting itself performed poorly. Goodhart (2018) explains that velocity proved to be unstable, and the BoE was unable to forecast or to control the preferred measure for the stock of money. Moreover, doubts were cast over which was the "best" measure for the money stock to track, and subsequent changes in the target measure were not helpful to maintain credibility. This led the UK to return to a form of exchange rate pegging, first shadowing the German D-mark and thereafter formally joining the European Exchange Rate Mechanism (ERM). When the UK left the ERM in September 1992, a new type of monetary policy strategy had become available and was considered "state-of-the-art" in the form of inflation targeting, which was soon adopted by the BoE (Goodhart, 2018).

2.1.3   Inflation targeting

Apart from the BoE, several other central banks introduced inflation targeting as their monetary policy strategy since it had been pioneered in 1989 in New Zealand. For instance, central banks in Australia, Canada, New Zealand, Norway, Sweden, and in several emerging and developing countries (such as Brazil, Indonesia and South Africa) apply this strategy.

Inflation targeting (hereafter IT) has three characteristics: (i) an announced numerical inflation target; (ii) monetary policy decisions are primarily based on differences between inflation forecasts and this numerical target; and (iii) a high degree of transparency and accountability.

As IT most often implies a distinctive forward-looking decision-making process, it has also become known as *inflation-forecast targeting* (Svensson, 1997). It means that the central bank sets its policy instruments in such a way that its inflation forecast (after some time) equals the inflation target. Central banks using this approach communicate monetary policy decisions in terms of a reaction to deviations in a forecast for inflation from the inflation target at a particular horizon. The central bank's forecast for inflation is therefore centrepiece both when it comes to decision-making and in communicating to the public (see Box 2.1).

BOX 2.1   HOW THE SWEDISH CENTRAL BANK TAKES A POLICY DECISION

The forecasting work prior to each monetary policy meeting begins with the Riksbank's staff analysing new data and events in the economy. Staff then produces a main forecast for how inflation, the policy rate and the economy are expected to develop. This work is carried out with the aid of various models. The models are used primarily to produce alternative forecasts for the repo rate, inflation and the economy. These alternative scenarios show how developments will be if specific events in the economy occur or if monetary policy is conducted differently than is assumed in the main forecast. At a relatively early stage of the process staff presents its forecast alternatives to the Executive Board in a meeting known as the Monetary Policy Group. At this meeting, there is a discussion between the members of the Executive Board and staff on the main forecast and the alternative scenarios.

Afterwards, staff continues its work and compiles a document that is a first draft of the Monetary Policy Report. This document is revised at a meeting of the Executive Board, where the Executive Board continues to discuss the various alternative forecasts and how they will be communicated in the Monetary Policy Report. The editorial work on the Monetary Policy Report continues, but after the monetary policy meeting the final adjustments are made to the text. The Monetary Policy Report is published on the Riksbank's website at the same time as the decision on the policy rate is published, normally the day after the monetary policy meeting.

On the basis of the work described above, the Executive Board establishes its joint view of what is considered a well-balanced monetary policy, considering inflation and the developments in the real economy during the forecast period. Naturally, there are occasionally differences of opinion in the Executive Board as to how inflation and the real economy will develop and thereby as to what would be a well-balanced monetary policy. In these cases, it is the majority view that is expressed in the decision and in the Monetary Policy Reports.

Source: https://www.riksbank.se/en-gb/monetary-policy/the-path-to-a -monetary-policy-decision/.

Inflation targeting does not imply that the central bank only cares about price stability. Stabilization of economic activity around its trend can be considered as well. That is why central banks often refer to their strategy as *flexible inflation targeting*. Drawing on the website of the Reserve Bank of Australia, this can be explained as follows. Economic growth tends to fluctuate around a long-term trend. This fluctuation is called the business cycle (see Figure 2.1). When the economy grows slowly relative to trend because of weak demand, the central bank can lower interest rates to stimulate economic growth and employment (see section 2.3 for a discussion as to how monetary policy affects the economy). On the other hand, when the economy grows too quickly relative to trend because of excessively strong demand, the central bank can raise interest rates to dampen economic activity and contain inflation.

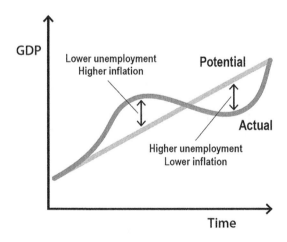

Figure 2.1   The business cycle

Source: https://www.rba.gov.au/education/resources/explainers/what-is -monetary-policy.html

Sometimes it might be difficult to achieve both price stability and low unemployment at the same time with monetary policy. This is why many central banks have adopted a "flexible medium-term inflation target". According to the Reserve Bank of Australia (source in Figure 2.1), this approach allows the central bank "to address short-run trade-offs that may occur between economic growth, employment and inflation. For example, there could be occasions when inflation might be too high at the same time that economic growth is too low and unemployment is too high. In these cases, the Reserve Bank must carefully consider the trade-off between smoothing the business cycle (in particular economic growth and unemployment) in the short run and achieving its inflation target. If inflation is too high, raising interest rates will help to bring inflation back towards the target, but will also be likely to reduce economic growth and put upward pressure on unemployment, all else being equal."

Whereas currently many central banks have some type of inflation targeting strategy in place, the framework is not undisputed. For example, former Bank of England governor Mervyn King (2021) argued that, when uncertainty is high and trust in the central bank is low, the anchoring properties of an inflation target are weak and monetary variables gain in importance for the inflation process.

2.2   MONETARY STRATEGY REVIEWS

After the Global Financial Crisis in 2008/09, in many countries a discussion emerged regarding central bank mandates (Table 2.2). According to a survey by Blinder *et al.* (2017) among 55 governors of central banks, in about half of the sample countries, discussions outside the central bank took place about changing the central bank mandate. Interestingly, discussions inside the central bank took place more often. The change most frequently discussed, both internally and externally, is adding a financial stability objective to the mandate. This issue will be discussed in Chapter 3. Changing the inflation target was also mentioned by a number of governors.

Within their established legal mandates, several major central banks have engaged in a formal review of their monetary policy strategy in recent years. For some central banks, like the Bank of Canada, such reviews are

Table 2.2   Discussions about central bank mandates after the
            financial crisis

	Discussions outside central bank		Discussions inside central bank	
	Yes	No or difficult to say	Yes	No or difficult to say
If yes, discussion about:	49%	51%	62%	38%
Inflation target	30%		21%	
Replace objective	11%		6%	
Add objective	56%		50%	
Other	37%		56%	

Notes: The left-hand side of the table shows whether, according to central bank governors, a discussion took place outside (inside) the central bank about changing the mandate. In answering the question as to what discussion took place, governors could tick several options. That is why the percentages do not add up to 100. The explanations provided in the survey indicate that, when governors answer "other", they mostly refer to discussions on adding financial stability.
Source: Blinder et al. (2017).

part of a regular cycle in which an agreement between the central bank and the government on how the mandate is best pursued is renewed every five years. For other central banks, structural changes in the economy and lessons learned over time about the functioning of the economy provided grounds to assess to what extent established frameworks were still fit-for-purpose to pursue legally assigned mandates. In particular, since the Global Financial Crisis many central banks have become confronted with policy rates at or close to their effective lower bound (see section 2.3.2 for a discussion) requiring the deployment of new, unconventional policy measures, and spells of inflation persistently below target, pushing them to review the aptness of their strategies in place. This section discusses recent reviews and changes to the monetary policy strategy of the Federal Reserve, the European Central Bank and the Bank of England.

The Fed announced its first ever public monetary policy strategy review in late 2018 as a means to assess how best to pursue its congressionally assigned mandate of maximum employment and price stability. The review was concluded in mid-2020 with the publication of a revised version of the Fed's statement on its longer-run goals and monetary policy strategy.[4] In its revised statement, the Fed reconfirmed its inflation target of 2 per cent, but added that, to anchor longer-term inflation expectations at the target level, it seeks to achieve inflation that averages 2 per cent over time. In other words, the Fed notes that its monetary policy will likely aim to achieve inflation moderately above 2 per cent for some time following periods when inflation has been running persistently below 2 per cent. Moreover, the Fed acknowledged that sustainably achieving its mandate depends on a stable financial system and, therefore, its assessment of the outlook will include an assessment of risks to the financial system that could be detrimental to its goals. Finally, the Fed expressed that it expects that the level of policy rates that is consistent with its mandate of maximum employment and price stability has declined relative to its historical average (see section 4.1 for a discussion). Against this backdrop, the Fed expects that its policy rates will be constrained by the effective lower bound more often than in the past adding to the risks that inflation can also be too low requiring the use of monetary policy instruments beyond policy rates.

The ECB announced its first encompassing monetary policy strategy review since 2003 in early 2020. The review was concluded in July 2021 with the publication of a monetary policy strategy statement.[5] In this statement, the ECB acknowledged that profound structural changes to the global economy had taken place since its last review in 2003, including a decline in trend growth and the legacy of the Global Financial Crisis, which have contributed to lower equilibrium interest rates (see section 4.1 for a discussion). In addition, it refers to structural trends such as globalization, digitalization and demographic factors that have complicated the conduct of monetary policy and contributed to inflation being persistently below target (see section 4.3 for a further discussion). Moreover, the ECB acknowledges in its strategy statement that financial stability is a precondition for price stability. In response to these challenges, the ECB decided to amend its price stability aim of inflation below, but close to 2 per cent in the medium term, to a symmetric price stability target of 2 per cent. Cognizant of the effective lower bound on interest rates, the ECB notes that, to maintain the symmetric inflation target, the monetary policy response may need to be especially forceful or persistent in order to avoid negative deviations from the inflation target becoming entrenched.

In addition, the ECB announced that it continues to stand ready to use other monetary policy instruments than policy rates, including forward guidance, asset purchases and longer-term refinancing operations (see sections 2.3 and 2.4). Finally, acknowledging the implications of climate change for price stability through its impact on the economy and the financial system, the ECB has announced a climate-related action plan, to incorporate climate factors into its monetary policy assessments and the design of its monetary policy operational framework (see section 4.4 for further discussion).

The BoE has its detailed objectives—or remit—specified at least once per year through a letter by the Chancellor of the Exchequer being sent to the BoE governor. The last broad review of the monetary policy framework in the UK was held in 2013 and led to several changes in the remit. First, since 2013, the remit acknowledges that in the short term there may be trade-offs between keeping inflation at target and other factors such as undesirable output volatility and financial stability considerations. In particular, the remit asks the BoE in those circumstances to communicate clearly about the policy actions that are taken and the trade-offs that have been made in determining the scale and duration of any expected deviation of inflation from the target. In addition, since 2013 the remit includes a section on unconventional policy instruments, recognizing that, in the event of exceptional shocks that result in policy rates reaching the effective lower bound, the BoE may deploy other tools if necessary. This includes asset purchases, lending schemes and forward guidance (see section 2.4.2). Changes to the remit after 2013 have been minor, though not all insignificant. Notably, in the letter accompanying the 2015 remit, it was clarified that the BoE's inflation target of 2 per cent is a symmetric target, i.e., that deviations below the target are to be treated in the same way as deviations above the target, ensuring there is no downward inflation bias in the framework. More recently, in 2021, the remit was updated to reflect the UK government's commitment to balanced growth that is also environmentally sustainable and consistent with the transition to a net zero emission economy.

Several common elements emerge from the reviews of monetary policy strategies that have been completed by the Fed, the ECB and the BoE. First, all three central banks recognize that the optimal design of the monetary policy strategy depends on the structural characteristics of the economy and can change over time, which is reflected in recent amendments of strategies. In this context, the three central banks acknowledge that there are interactions between monetary policy and other policy areas, all of them explicitly referencing financial stability in their strategy and two out of three referring to climate change (see also section 4.4). After the conclusion of their reviews, both the Fed and the ECB announced that in the future they intend to complete similar reviews more regularly, at fixed intervals of around five years. Second, all central banks have redesigned their strategy in a way acknowledging that inflation that is too low can be as undesirable as inflation that is too high. This has led them to move to and/or emphasize the symmetry of their targets, even though the exact specificities differ across central banks. Third, the three central banks confirm that there can be circumstances that require the toolkit of monetary policy to be extended to instruments beyond policy rates, a topic that will be explored in more detail in the next section.

2.3   MONETARY POLICY INSTRUMENTS

As discussed, in most jurisdictions monetary policy is about maintaining price stability, in other words maintaining the purchasing power of money. Despite the field alluding by name to "money", different from many traditional textbooks and in past regimes of monetary targeting, money and monetary indicators no longer play a leading role in the conduct of contemporary monetary policy. Against this backdrop, this book refrains from outlining the traditional framework of banks as "monetary financial institutions" that explains how banks play a key role in the creation of the broader money supply in the economy as it is no longer critical to understand how central banks implement monetary policy. Interested readers can familiarize themselves with this topic by reading the excellent explanation provided in Bundesbank (2017).

2.3.1   Conventional monetary policy

In the two decades leading up to the Global Financial Crisis, most central banks in advanced economies typically implemented monetary policy by steering short-term interest rates in the economy. To simplify, they raised or lowered money market rates through the use of their instruments if inflation and economic developments so required, i.e., raising interest rates if inflation becomes too high and lowering interest rates if the economic outlook deteriorates. Economists usually describe central bank policies by the Taylor rule, as explained in Box 2.2.

BOX 2.2   THE TAYLOR RULE[6]

The Taylor rule is a simple way to describe monetary policy by linking the policy rate to deviations of inflation from its target and of output from its potential (the output gap). In other words, the Taylor rule is a descriptive reaction function of the central bank, showing how it responds to economic developments. Taylor (1993) proposed the following rule:

$$i_t = r^* + \pi^* + k_\pi (\pi_t - \pi^*) + k_x x_t$$

where i_t is referred to as the Taylor-rule rate in period t, r^* is the equilibrium real interest rate (see section 4.1), $\pi_t - \pi^*$ is the deviation of inflation in period t from the inflation target π^*, and x_t is the output gap in period t. Taylor suggested the following values for the coefficients: $r^* = 2$, $\pi^* = 2$, $k_\pi = 1.5$ and $k_x = 0.5$. The specification described the policy of the Federal Reserve over the period 1987–1992 surprisingly well. Taylor had not estimated the relationship, but subsequent studies estimated the model in order to describe the behaviour of central banks.[7] So, in contrast to Taylor (1993), these studies estimate the key parameters of interest, i.e., k_π and k_x, where it is important that the inflation reaction coefficient is larger than 1 as that ensures real interest rates respond in a stabilizing way to inflationary pressures.

However, as Svensson (2003) has shown, a simple Taylor rule will not be optimal in a plausible macroeconomic model. Interest rate changes affect inflation and output with a sizeable lag. Therefore, monetary policy needs to be forward-looking in practice, i.e., interest rate decisions should be based on *expected* inflation and output. Forecasts of future inflation and output deviations from the central bank's targets are used in optimizing the path of the central bank interest rate.[8] Realized outcomes for inflation and output may enter the optimal decision rule if they help to predict future inflation and output, but so will any other variable that provides information concerning future inflation and output. Consequently, monetary policy will, in general, be more complicated than the simple Taylor rule suggests. As Bernanke (2015b) argues:

> The simplicity of the Taylor rule disguises the complexity of the underlying judgments that FOMC members must continually make if they are to make good

policy decisions. Here are just a few examples (not an exhaustive list): The Taylor rule assumes that policy-makers know, and can agree on, the size of the output gap. In fact, as current debates about the amount of slack in the labour market attest, measuring the output gap is very difficult and FOMC members typically have different judgments. […] The Taylor rule provides no guidance about what to do when the predicted rate is negative, as has been the case for almost the entire period since the crisis. There is no agreement on what the Taylor rule weights on inflation and the output gap should be from a prescriptive optimal policy perspective, except with respect to their signs. The optimal weights would respond not only to changes in preferences of policy-makers, but also to changes in the structure of the economy and the channels of monetary policy transmission.

To understand how central banks can change short-term interest rates, we have to explain in somewhat more detail how the market for central bank reserves works. The demand for reserves stems from banks needing to make payments, which they do by debiting or crediting their account at the central bank. The central bank determines the supply of reserves. Traditionally, this is done in such a way that the market interest rate on reserves, the price on the market as determined by supply and demand, is in line with the central bank's preferred level of this interest rate, i.e., the interest rate that is deemed consistent with the central bank's objective.

In a *corridor system*, this market rate is between a floor and a ceiling. The floor is the interest rate the central bank pays on reserves, i.e., on the banks' deposits at the central bank. Banks that hold more central bank reserves than they need for payment and precautionary purposes will try to lend those to banks in need of liquidity. But they have no incentive to accept an interest rate on an overnight loan to another bank below the rate offered by the central bank that, thus, serves as a floor for the interest rate on the market for overnight reserves. The ceiling banks are willing to accept is determined by the interest rate that the central bank charges if a bank lends from the central bank (often called the *discount rate*). Banks with a liquidity shortage for payment and precautionary purposes will try to borrow from other banks, but they have no incentive to borrow at interest rates higher than the one charged by the central bank. As a consequence, all market activity is contained within the corridor.

By changing the supply of reserves, central banks can steer the market interest rate. For instance, central banks can buy or sell government bonds on the secondary government bond market. This is known as open market operations. The central bank adds reserves into the banking system by buying government bonds or removes reserves by selling government bonds. Central banks may also use *repurchase agreements* (or repos for short), or refinancing operations to perform open market operations. A repo is a transaction that occurs in two parts. In the first part, the central bank sells a bond to a bank, resulting in a decrease in reserves on that day. In the pre-arranged second part, at an agreed price and date in the future, the central bank receives the bond back, resulting in an increase of the supply of reserves on that day. In the opposite case, commonly referred to as a "reverse repo", the central commences the transaction by buying a bond, and providing reserves to the bank. The second leg of this transaction involves the central bank returning the bond to the bank, resulting in a decrease in the supply of reserves on that day. *Refinancing operations* are collateralized loans to banks. So, the central bank provides liquidity to commercial banks but to protect the central bank from losses, collateral is required. The ECB used this instrument to carry out open market operations. They could be carried out with full or partial allotment. In the event of *full allotment*, all bids by commercial banks were honoured. In the event of *partial allotment*, a choice was made between a fixed-rate and a variable-rate tender. If a *fixed-rate tender* was chosen, all banks paid the main refinancing rate. If a *variable-rate tender* was opted for, the highest bidders (starting from a minimum bid rate) were to be allotted the loan first.

Central banks can also change interest rates by altering their policy rates, i.e., shifting the corridor up or down by changing the interest rate that banks have to pay if they borrow from the central bank and the interest rate the central bank pays on deposits of commercial banks at the central bank. The market interest moves then in the same direction.

Figure 2.2 illustrates the corridor system for the case of the Reserve Bank of Australia (RBA) before unconventional policies were introduced. The policy interest rate corridor is defined by a floor and a ceiling around the cash rate target in the Australian cash market. The floor is the RBA's deposit rate, which was the cash rate less 0.1 and later 0.25 percentage points on balances that banks deposit at the RBA. The ceiling is the RBA's lending rate, which was the cash rate plus 0.1 and later 0.25 percentage points, banks had to pay if they borrow from the RBA to cover shortfalls.

Many other central banks also had a corridor system. This also holds true for the Federal Reserve. Prior to October 2008, the Fed operated a corridor-type system with the interest-on-reserves rate set to zero. However, since 2008, the Federal Reserve has implemented monetary

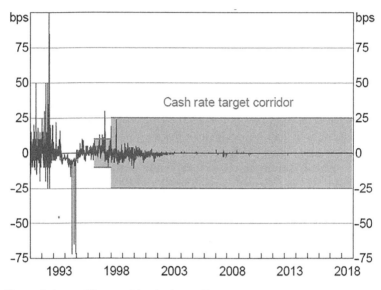

Figure 2.2   The corridor in Australia

Source: https://www.rba.gov.au/education/resources/teacher-updates/bridging -the-textbook-gaps-on-how-the-rba-implements-monetary-policy/index.html

policy through a *floor system*. In this system, banks have an excess of reserves, and the Fed pays interest on those reserves at a rate termed the interest on excess reserves (IOER) rate. The large supply of reserves means that there are many potential lenders and few borrowers, pushing the federal funds rate, i.e., the rate at which banks and certain other institutions borrow and lend with each other, down close to the IOER rate (the "floor" below which banks are better off depositing with the Fed than lending). Hence, the Fed can change the federal funds rate simply by changing IOER. Likewise, since 2015, the corridor system of the ECB has de facto evolved into a floor system. In the case of both the Fed and the ECB, the increase in the supply of reserves causing the transition from a corridor to a floor system can be associated with the use of unconventional monetary policy tools (see section 2.3.2).

Figure 2.3 compares the floor and corridor systems. The left-hand side panel of the figure shows a corridor-style system. The discount rate (the rate against which banks can borrow from the central bank) is set above the target interest rate and the interest-on-reserves rate is set below it. Open market operations are then used as needed to change the supply of reserve balances so that the market interest rate is as close as possible to the target. This approach relies on setting the supply of reserves so that it falls in the inelastic region of the demand curve. The right-hand side panel of the figure depicts a floor-type system. In this approach, the interest-on-reserves rate is set very close or equal to the target rate. In this case, the appropriate supply of reserves falls in the elastic region of the demand curve and the market rate is close to the floor created by the interest-on-reserves rate.

2.3.2   Unconventional monetary policy

Typically, central bank policy rates have been positive for most of history

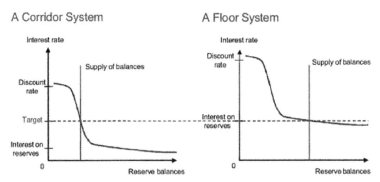

Figure 2.3   Corridor and floor system

Source: Keister (2018).

across most central banks. However, in June 2014 and again in September 2014, the ECB lowered the deposit facility rate by 10 bps each time to minus 0.2 per cent. After further decreases in 2015, 2016 and 2019, in 2021 it stood at minus 0.5 per cent. A negative interest rate on its deposit facility implies that the ECB charges banks to deposit their surplus liquidity in their accounts at the ECB. The ECB was the first major central bank to introduce negative interest rates; those from smaller countries such as

Denmark and Switzerland had taken this step earlier. The Bank of Japan has implemented a negative policy rate at minus 0.1 per cent as of 2016. By contrast, policy rates of the Fed and the BoE have remained positive, the former having lowered its policy rate to a range of 0 per cent to 0.25 per cent and the latter to 0.1 per cent.

There are limits as to how far the central bank can lower its policy rates to stimulate the economy. This is because the nominal short-term interest rate cannot be lowered (much) below zero, the so-called *effective lower bound*. This lower bound reflects the fact that economic agents will prefer to keep funds in the form of cash rather than deposit them at a bank that charges negative rates on deposits (i.e., customers are charged to deposit their money). Or, when policy rates would drop below a specific threshold, banks and other financial intermediaries would tighten lending standards in order to avoid losses, defeating the purpose of lower policy rates (Brunnermeier and Koby, 2018). The exact level of the effective lower bound is uncertain and can depend *inter alia* on the carry cost of cash, the balance sheet structure of the financial system, and how long very low policy rates are put in place.

When policy rates are at their effective lower bound, central banks have other instruments at their disposal to stimulate the economy, most notably asset purchase programmes, often referred to as quantitative easing (QE). As pointed out by Borio and Disyatat (2010), the distinguishing feature of these measures is that the central bank actively uses its balance sheet to affect market prices and financial conditions beyond a short-term interest rate.

The Bank of Japan was the first of the central banks in major advanced countries to introduce QE. Since the early 1990s, Japan's inflation rate has been persistently low and was even negative in some periods. The BoJ adopting various QE programmes, at first for relatively moderate amounts (in the period 2001–2006) and, later, for much larger amounts (after the Global Financial Crisis). The BoJ introduced a new Quantitative and Qualitative Monetary Easing (QQE) programme in April 2013, with a very high volume of public and private asset purchases pushing the size of the central bank's balance sheet to above 100 per cent of GDP. Despite this sizeable monetary easing, inflation did not achieve a lasting increase and remained extremely low (Borrallo Egea and del Río López, 2021).[9]

After the Federal Open Market Committee (FOMC) of the Federal Reserve had lowered the target for the federal funds rate to a range of 0 to 25 basis points in December 2008, US policy-makers faced the challenge of how to further ease the stance of monetary policy as the economic outlook deteriorated. The Federal Reserve decided to purchase substantial quantities of assets with medium and long maturities in an effort to drive down private (long-term) borrowing rates.

The BoE began buying bonds through QE in March 2009 as a response to the Global Financial Crisis. According to the BoE website, "To date we have bought £895 billion worth of bonds through QE. Most of that sum (£875 billion) has been used to buy U.K. government bonds. A much smaller part (£20 billion) has been used to buy U.K. corporate bonds."[10]

The ECB introduced QE much later than most other central banks in major advanced countries. Initially, its unconventional policies during the financial crisis mainly focused on supporting lending via the banking sector. The main reason is that the banking sector plays a fundamental role in the monetary transmission mechanism in the euro area, because non-financial corporations are highly depending on bank credit. The ECB provided, for instance, unlimited liquidity through "fixed-rate tenders with full allotment". Thus, contrary to normal practice, banks had unlimited access to central bank liquidity at the main refinancing rate, subject to adequate collateral. After inflation in the euro area had dropped below 0 per cent and the medium-term outlook for inflation remained persistently below target, the ECB launched an expanded asset purchase programme (APP), encompassing its existing purchase programmes for asset-backed securities and covered bonds and a new purchase programme for sovereign bonds, in January 2015.

Former FOMC Chair Ben Bernanke once famously quipped that "the problem with QE is [that] it works in practice, but [not] in theory."[11] This comment reflected the fact that, in many traditional economic models developed before the crisis central bank balance sheet operations had no material impact on macroeconomic outcomes. This result can be traced back to specific characteristics of many pre-crisis models. In these models either there was no heterogeneity in different types of financial assets that economic agents can hold, or there was (either explicit or implicit) an assumption of complete financial markets and perfect substitutability between different types of assets. In practice, however, these conditions are likely not to be satisfied, for example, as a consequence of investor preferences for financial assets with specific characteristics, transaction costs and other market imperfections that can become amplified in times of financial market distress. These factors give rise to different types of premia on financial assets, including term premia, credit risk premia and liquidity premia. Central banks can be effective in easing broader financing conditions with QE by absorbing assets with specific risk exposures, which will lower risk premia. Typically, central banks design QE in such a way that it is targeted at reducing the term premium, by purchasing longer-term government bonds (i.e., bonds that are generally assessed to be exposed to duration risk and only to a limited extent to other sources of risk). However, there are also examples of asset purchase programmes where central banks target different sources of risk, e.g., by purchasing corporate bonds.

Apart from negative interest rates and QE, central banks have also introduced unconventional monetary policy instruments that explicitly target bank lending. For instance, the ECB introduced *targeted longer-term refinancing operations* (TLTROs). In this scheme, the amount banks can borrow from the ECB is linked to their loans to non-financial corporations and households. These operations offer banks long-term funding at attractive conditions to further ease private sector credit conditions and stimulate bank lending to the real economy. A similar scheme, called the *Funding for Lending Scheme* (FLS), was launched by the Bank of England in July 2012. It is designed to encourage banks to expand their lending to households and private non-financial corporates, by providing funds at cheaper rates than those prevailing in current markets. Both the quantity and the price of these funds are linked to the amount of lending that banks do.

Whereas the measures discussed in this section were considered unconventional when they were first deployed, meanwhile they have become more mainstream across central banks. In particular, in response to the COVID-19 pandemic, many central banks introduced several emergency measures, including unprecedented asset purchase programmes (see section 3.4 for a discussion). In addition to using conventional and unconventional monetary policy tools, central banks can shape market expectations by their public announcements.

2.4   CENTRAL BANK COMMUNICATION

2.4.1   Introduction

Central bank communication can be defined as the provision of information by the central bank to the public on the objectives of monetary policy, the monetary policy strategy, the economic outlook and the outlook for future policy decisions (Blinder *et al.*, 2008). Central banks can choose from a large menu of communication instruments, such as press releases, speeches, official reports and interviews, and each central bank uses its own mixture. Nowadays, central banks provide a lot more information than they used to do in the past. This reflects not only the call for greater transparency and accountability as discussed in section 1.4, but also the view that (1) central bank communication may enhance the way financial markets work and process information about the outlook for the economy and monetary policy, and (2) central bank communication can be used by central banks as an instrument of monetary policy.

As to the first point: the idea is that central bank communication would make policy more predictable and market expectations of future short rates more accurate. The central bank's policy reaction function should be so well understood that all the relevant news for financial markets would stem from developments in the economy, not from the actions or words of the central bank. Research has shown convincingly that the predictability of the interest rate decisions of the major central banks has improved remarkably in recent years. In fact, financial markets' expectations nowadays are generally well aligned with actual decisions (Blinder *et al.*, 2008).

The view that central bank communication can be used as an instrument of monetary policy is based on the insight that monetary policy to a very large extent is "management of expectations" (Svensson, 2006). Communication about monetary policy is a way to manage expectations.[12] Even though central banks only have direct full control over the current short-term interest rate, they can use communication to influence expectations about the future path of short-term interest rates, thereby affecting long-term interest rates. Abstracting from risk premia, long-term interest rates, reflecting expected future short-term interest rates, affect saving and investment decisions by households and firms. Therefore, financial markets' and the broader public's perception of future policy rates is critical for the way in which monetary policy impacts the economy

(Blinder *et al.*, 2008). In addition, central bank communication may affect inflation expectations. Inflation expectations are important, as they will affect actual inflation. In a very simple model, if economic agents are forward-looking and expect an inflation rate of, say, 2 percent and behave accordingly, actual inflation will tend to move towards this rate, because agents will incorporate it in their wage- and price-setting behaviour. *Anchoring of inflation expectations*, i.e., inflation expectations being in line with the inflation target of the central bank, prevents a fall in nominal short-term interest rates to be associated with a medium-term weakening of the economic situation and thus a decline in inflation expectations. For these reasons, central banks aim to "anchor" inflation expectations.

As it became increasingly clear that managing expectations is a useful part of monetary policy, communication policy became an important instrument in the central banker's toolkit. At the Federal Reserve, for example, then Chairman Alan Greenspan tried in 2003 to manage expectations by communicating consistently that the Fed would keep the federal funds rate low "for a considerable period." This was one step in a long march towards greater transparency that began in February 1994 when the FOMC first started announcing its decisions on the federal funds rate target. (Before, financial markets had to figure out themselves what the FOMC had decided.) Other important steps included publishing voting, with names attached, immediately after each FOMC meeting. In January 2012, the Fed publicly announced its inflation target and started publishing the so-called "dot plot", which provides FOMC members' assessments of future "appropriate monetary policy".

2.4.2   Forward guidance[13]

One important form of central bank communication that has become very popular is *forward guidance*, i.e., communicating about the future path of monetary policy. The reason is straightforward. Monetary policy works not only through the current setting of policy instruments, but also through expectations about the future course of policy, which affects, among other things, the shape of the term structure of interest rates. Management of these expectations can therefore be a powerful tool once the central bank has already lowered short-term rates as much as it can.

Drawing on Den Haan (2013), we can explain this as follows. In recent years, central banks have frequently reduced the policy interest rate to the lowest possible level—the effective lower bound (ELB), which may be negative. Through forward guidance, monetary policy may be effective even if the central bank cannot cut current policy rates any further. If a central bank can credibly commit to future values of the policy rate, it can work around the ELB constraint by promising monetary accommodation in the future once the ELB ceases to bind. Figure 2.4 explains this. The solid line in the figure shows what would happen to the policy rate under the central bank's normal strategy (i.e., without forward guidance). T_0 is the current period. The central bank would prefer a negative policy rate given the economic situation, but it cannot reduce its rate further. In period T, the economy has recovered to the extent that the bank's reaction function no longer calls for a negative policy interest rate. Now suppose that the central bank could lower the expected values of future (strictly positive) interest rates. The long-term interest rate reflects expected future short-term rates. So, reducing expected future policy rates would reduce the long-term interest rate in the current period, which would stimulate contemporaneous consumption and investment. The central bank can accomplish lower long-term interest rates by promising to keep the policy interest rate "lower for longer". The corresponding time path is the dashed line in Figure 2.4. The policy interest rate remains at zero until T^* and then catches up to the level that is in line with the bank's preferred policy.

However, there is a time-inconsistency problem because between T and T^*, the central bank's preferred policy is to have a positive interest rate, whereas the bank had promised to keep the interest rate at zero during this period. So, the central bank has an incentive to break its promise. And if markets believe the central bank will not stick to its promise, they will not adjust their expectations of future policy rates downward so that long-term rates will not come down. In other words, this forward guidance policy can only be effective if the central bank can convince markets that—like Odysseus who in Greek mythology tied himself to the mast to withstand the song of the Sirens—it is committed to this policy and will not change course.

Apart from *Odyssean forward guidance*, central banks may apply *Delphic forward guidance*. This means that central banks publish their forecasts of macroeconomic developments and their likely monetary policy actions without any commitment. So, the central bank acts in a similar way as the Delphic oracle, hence its name. However, this type of forward guidance also may affect private sector expectations. As long-term rates are more relevant for economic decisions than the current level of the overnight rate, any action by the central bank that influences interest rate expectations could be a potential tool of monetary policy, even if current short-term rates cannot be reduced any further (Blinder *et al.*, 2008). In summary, whereas Odyssean forward guidance is about credibly committing to deviate from the central banks' reaction function in order to provide more policy accommodation, Delphic forward guidance is about clarifying the input that the central bank responds to without adapting or deviating from its predetermined reaction function.

In practice, central banks apply three broad forms of forward guidance: (1) *qualitative* (or open-ended) *forward guidance*, where the central bank does not provide detailed quantitative information about the envisaged time frame for its policy intentions; (2) *calendar-based* (or

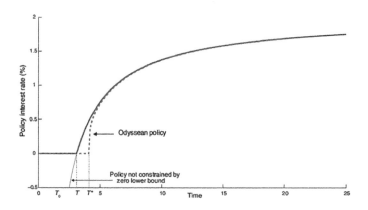

Figure 2.4   The effect of forward guidance

Source: Den Haan (2013).

time-contingent) *forward guidance*, where the central bank refers to a clearly specified time horizon for its policies; and (3) *threshold-based* (or data-based, state-contingent) *forward guidance*, where the central bank links future rates to specific quantitative economic thresholds. Figure 2.5, which is based on a survey among central bank governors, shows that all types of forward guidance are widely used. In fact, central banks often use more than one type of forward guidance.

The Bank of Japan was a pioneer in using open-ended forward guidance. In 1999, it announced that interest rates would stay at zero until deflationary concerns were dispelled. When it faced deflationary pressure in 2013, the BoJ again relied on forward guidance, stipulating a 2-year period to

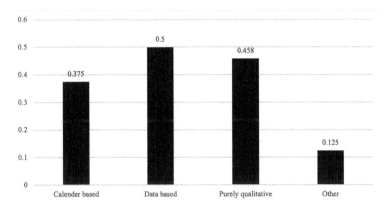

Figure 2.5   Use of different types of forward guidance by central banks

Source: Blinder *et al.* (2017).

achieve the objective of a 2 per cent inflation rate (Den Haan, 2013).

When the Bank of England introduced its forward guidance in August 2013 based on a threshold for unemployment, it announced that the guidance would cease to hold if some knockout conditions were satisfied. However, the unexpectedly strong decline in unemployment to below the threshold forced the BoE to change its forward guidance as early as May 2014. Despite the increased levels of economic activity, the MPC was still worried about the slack in the economy. According to the minutes of the MPC, all members agreed that, "in the absence of other inflationary pressures, it would be necessary to see more evidence of slack reducing before an increase in Bank Rate would be warranted." This example illustrates that, even though forward guidance can be a very powerful tool, it may also create a lot of confusion if economic developments are very different than expected. Under those circumstances, the credibility of the central bank may even be undermined.

The Fed has used different types of forward guidance. For instance, in December 2008, its FOMC announced, "[t]he Committee anticipates that weak economic conditions are likely to warrant exceptionally low levels of the federal funds rate for some time." In March 2009, "for some time" was replaced by "for an extended period". In August 2011, the Fed switched from open-ended to time-contingent forward guidance, and in December 2012 it shifted to state-contingent forward guidance.

The ECB's forward guidance has mostly been open ended. While after previous Governing Council meetings the ECB had stated that monetary policy would be accommodative "for as long as necessary", in July 2013 the ECB announced that interest rates would remain at present or lower levels for "an extended period of time". More recently, the ECB's forward guidance on interest rates has become increasingly state dependent. For example, when it amended its forward guidance after the conclusion of its strategy review (see section 2.2), the ECB specified a number of conditions for inflation and underlying inflation that needed to be satisfied before the policy rate would be increased.[14]

Not everyone is convinced about the usefulness of forward guidance. Former BoE governor Mervyn King (2021) argues,

> central banks have been giving "forward guidance" that interest rates will remain close to or below zero for the indefinite future. This policy stance relies heavily on the assumptions that expectations drive inflation, and central banks drive expectations. In other words, longer-term inflation is determined by the official inflation target. ... In the models that have come to dominate central-bank thinking, inflation is pinned down by a central-bank "reaction function" which guarantees that interest rates or QE will be set so as to ensure that inflation returns to target. But in a world of radical uncertainty, where none of us know[s] the true dynamics of the economy, we cannot be confident that central banks will in fact behave in a way consistent with hitting the inflation target. In such a world, our expectations are too fragile to anchor inflation.

2.5   MONETARY POLICY TRANSMISSION

The monetary transmission mechanism consists of the various channels through which conventional and unconventional monetary policy actions affect the economy and the inflation outlook in particular. Figure 2.6 shows these channels in a schematic way.

Under the *interest rate channel*, monetary policy influences output via the nominal interest rate. A tightening of monetary policy typically aims at

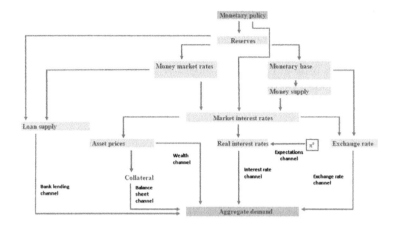

Figure 2.6   A schematic overview of monetary policy transmission

Source: Based on Kuttner and Mosser (2002).

increasing the costs for (commercial) banks' refinancing via central bank or interbank lending. Banks try to pass their higher refinancing costs through to their lending rates, which then reduces credit demand and lending. At the same time, the rise in money market rates is transmitted to other financial markets. The reason is that non-banks may try to switch to alternative means to borrow (e.g., corporate bonds) if bank lending becomes more expensive. The increased supply of corporate bonds increases interest rates on these securities as well.

The *bank lending channel* is based on the presumption that banks heavily rely on demand deposits as an important source of funding. Contractionary monetary policy induces a fall in these deposits, thus limiting banks' access to funding as banks cannot easily substitute to other (more expensive) forms of funding. This, in turn, will force banks to reduce the availability of bank loans. To the extent that a significant subset of firms and households relies heavily (or even exclusively) on bank financing, a reduction in loan supply will depress aggregate spending.

Interest rate changes also affect firms' balance sheets. An increase in interest rates lowers the net worth of their assets, which means a lower collateral value and thus a reduced ability to borrow (the *balance sheet channel*).

Likewise, under the *wealth channel*, consumption and investment are also affected by movements in asset prices. For example, when equity or house prices drop in response to monetary policy, households that own shares or a house become less wealthy and may choose to decrease their consumption.

The *expectations channel* works through the impact of monetary policy announcements on expectations of households and firms (see section 2.4). The central bank can, for instance, exert a powerful direct influence on price developments by guiding economic agents' expectations of future inflation, thereby influencing their spending and wage- and price-setting behaviour.

Monetary policy changes may also affect the exchange rate, which, in turn, will normally affect inflation in three ways (*exchange rate channel*). First, exchange rate movements may directly affect the domestic price of imported goods. If the exchange rate appreciates, the price of imported goods tends to fall, thus helping to directly reduce inflation. Second, if these imports are used as inputs into the production process, lower prices for inputs might, over time, lower the prices of final goods. Third, an appreciation in the exchange rate may make domestically produced goods less competitive on world markets, which tends to constrain external demand and thus reduce overall demand pressure in the economy. All else equal, an appreciation of the level of the exchange rate (due to exogenous or policy-induced factors) tends to reduce inflationary pressures, and vice versa.

In recent studies, it has been pointed out that low interest rates may induce financial institutions to take more risk (*risk-taking channel*). This channel is not shown in Figure 2.6. The channel is thought to operate mainly via two mechanisms. First, low interest rates boost asset and collateral values. This, in conjunction with the belief that the increase in asset values is sustainable, leads both borrowers and banks to accept higher risks. Second, low interest rates make riskier assets more attractive, as agents search for higher yields. For banks, these two effects usually translate into a softening of credit standards, which can lead to an excessive increase in loan supply.

NOTES

1. At https://www.riksbank.se/en-gb/monetary-policy/the-inflation-target/
2. Although the view that deflation is very costly is widely shared, Borio *et al.* (2015) question it. These authors test the historical link between output growth and deflation in a sample covering 140 years for up to 38 economies. Their evidence suggests that this link is weak and derives largely from the Great Depression.
3. If the level of aggregate output is at its potential level, as classical economists like Irving Fisher assumed, it can also be treated as reasonably constant in the short run. This implies that, if the money stock doubles, prices must also double in the short run. Hence, inflation is a monetary phenomenon. If output is not always at full potential, an increase in the money stock affects both output and prices.
4. At https://www.federalreserve.gov/monetarypolicy/files/fomc_longerrungoals .pdf
5. At https://www.ecb.europa.eu/home/search/review/html/ecb.strategyreview _monpol_strategy_statement.en.html
6. This box heavily draws on Gorter *et al.* (2008).
7. Sometimes the Taylor rule is not used to describe monetary policy, but to prescribe monetary policy. See Bernanke (2015b) for a further discussion.
8. See Wieland and Wolters (2013) for further discussion.
9. This prompted the BoJ to try new strategies. In January 2016, it introduced a negative interest rate policy for a part of banks' reserves at the central bank and, in September 2016, it adopted a yield curve control strategy: in addition to negative short-term interest rates, a 0 per cent target was set for 10-year Japanese Government Bond yields, complemented by the commitment to allow inflation to increase above the 2 per cent target and stay above this target in a stable manner for some time with the aim of anchoring inflation expectations at this level (Borrallo Egea and del Río López, 2021).
10. At https://www.bankofengland.co.uk/monetary-policy/quantitative-easing
11. At https://www.cnbc.com/2014/01/16/bernanke-cracks-wise-the-best-qe-joke -ever.html
12. These paragraphs draw heavily on Blinder *et al.* (2008) and de Haan and Sturm (2019).
13. This section heavily draws on de Haan *et al.* (2020) and Moessner *et al.* (2017).
14. Since July 2021, the ECB's forward guidance on policy rate is: "In support of its symmetric two per cent inflation target and in line with its monetary policy strategy, the Governing Council expects the key ECB interest rates to remain at their present or lower levels until it sees inflation reaching two per cent well ahead of the end of its projection horizon and durably for the rest

of the projection horizon, and it judges that realized progress in underlying inflation is sufficiently advanced to be consistent with inflation stabilising at two per cent over the medium term. This may also imply a transitory period in which inflation is moderately above target."

3. Financial stability and crisis management

3.1 INTRODUCTION

One of the main tasks of central banks is maintaining financial stability. As shown in Chapter 1, preventing financial crises and reducing the fall-out of crises have been important historical reasons for the creation of central banks. Traditionally, this was often understood as in Walter Bagehot's book *Lombard Street* (1873), which suggested that a central bank as a guarantor of financial stability should be a lender of last resort. By providing liquidity to illiquid but solvent banks, the central bank should avoid (or manage) banking panics. However, the lender of last resort function has evolved in line with financial market development (BIS, 2020). In modern financial systems, markets or financial institutions other than banks, may be subject to "runs" driven by similar underlying forces. This can trigger a self-reinforcing spiral that can lead to the breakdown of key financial institutions and markets.

In discussing what central banks can do to maintain financial stability, a distinction should be made between micro- and macro-prudential supervision. Micro-prudential supervision aims to limit the distress of individual financial institutions, with the ultimate objective of protecting their customers. It does not focus on the financial system as a whole. In contrast, macro-prudential supervision aims to limit financial system-wide distress, with the ultimate objective of protecting the overall economy from significant losses in output. A macro-prudential perspective is important, because even if all individual financial institutions look safe, there may still be serious risks to the financial system as a whole. For instance, if many banks have common exposures (say, a local real estate market), a shock (say, an increase in local unemployment) may affect all these banks at the same time.

This chapter is organized as follows. Section 3.2 first discusses the question of whether central banks should be responsible for micro-prudential supervision and then outlines micro-prudential supervision and the role of central banks therein. Section 3.3 discusses macro-prudential policies. Finally, section 3.4 zooms in on crisis management. During the Global Financial Crisis of 2007/08 and the European sovereign debt crisis, central banks stepped in, even to such an extent that they were criticized for stretching or even overstepping their mandate. During the recent crisis induced by the COVID-19 pandemic, central banks intervened on an unprecedented scale.

3.2   MICRO-PRUDENTIAL SUPERVISION: A TASK FOR CENTRAL BANKS?

Should central banks be responsible for micro-prudential supervision, i.e., the supervision of individual financial institutions? Goodhart and Schoenmaker (1995) identify the following pros and cons. The first argument in favour of separating financial supervision and monetary policy is the possibility of a conflict of interest if the same institution is responsible for both activities. A central bank that is responsible for supervision and, thus, also for failures of financial institutions, might be tempted to avoid such failures by admitting lower interest rates than would be consistent with maintaining price stability. In small, open economies that have a (more or less) fixed exchange rate (like the Netherlands had in the past), the probability of a conflict of interest between the two responsibilities is less likely. It is therefore not surprising that, say, the Dutch central bank became responsible for financial supervision, while in Germany a separate institution has the primary responsibility for supervision.

A second reason to separate the responsibilities is the bad publicity usually associated with failures or rescue operations of financial institutions. A loss of reputation might then affect the credibility of monetary policy. It may also affect central bank independence (discussed in section 1.3).

However, a separation of financial supervision and monetary policy may also have drawbacks. First, the central bank plays a crucial role in the smooth operation of the payments system and its associated financial risks. To limit these risks, the central bank may want to supervise and regulate the participants of the payments system. In addition, the central bank functions as a "lender of last resort" for the financial system; in this capacity, it has the task to provide liquidity to financial institutions facing a run or panic but that are still solvent. As shown in section 1.1, this responsibility played a key role in establishing the Fed (and many other central banks as well). If the central bank is also responsible for supervision, it may be in a better position to assess whether a financial institution is still solvent. Having all responsibilities under one roof has informational advantages and economies of scale.

The involvement of central banks in supervision has changed remarkably. Masciandaro and Romelli (2018) created a dataset containing information on the authorities responsible for the oversight of the financial sector (banking, insurance and financial markets) in a large sample of 105 countries over the 1996–2013 period. Their Central Bank Involvement in Supervision (CBIS) Index captures the degree of central bank involvement in financial supervision. Figure 3.1 shows the level of this index in 2006 and 2013, with darker shades corresponding to a higher number of sectors that fall under the central bank's supervisory responsibility. The figure shows a clear tendency towards assigning more supervisory powers to central banks. Masciandaro and Romelli (2018) also examine the determinants of reforms that increase the involvement of central banks in supervision of the entire financial sector. They find that banking crises significantly increase the probability that a country will reform its supervisory structure. This result is specific to financial sector turmoil and not to other types of crises, such as currency crises or economic recessions.[1]

Consistent with this view, after the 2007/08 financial crisis, the supervisory architecture in several countries has changed. In the UK, for instance, the responsibility for banking supervision had been allocated to the Financial Services Authority (FSA) which was charged with supervising all segments of the financial system since 1997, when the UK parliament voted to give the BoE operational independence with a clear objective of price stability. After the crisis, financial supervision was transferred back to the central bank. Nowadays, the Prudential Regulation Authority (PRA), a division of the BoE, is responsible for micro-prudential supervision.

Likewise, in the euro area the ECB became responsible for the supervision of banks after euro area political leaders had decided in June 2012 to establish a Banking Union. The background for this decision is as follows. The financial crisis had made it clear that having banking supervision as a national competence is inadequate in a currency union with a large banking sector and high interconnectedness among national banking systems and between banking systems and sovereigns.[2] Experience of the near failure of cross-border banks in Europe suggests that, in times of crisis, national authorities focus on preserving the national elements, while the integrated value of a bank is neglected (Gros and Schoenmaker, 2014). In the Banking Union, the Single Supervisory Mechanism (SSM), in which the ECB takes a leading role, has become responsible for micro-prudential supervision of banks in the euro area since November 2014.[3] Under the new system, the ECB directly supervises around 110 significant banking institutions, representing about 80 per cent of total banking assets in the euro area. The ECB indirectly supervises less significant banks in the participating countries, which number approximately 2,400 in the euro area. These banks continue to be directly supervised by the national competent authorities (national central banks or national supervisory authorities), but the ECB can decide at any time to take over the direct supervision of any of these banks. Setting up the SSM required changes to the ECB's organizational structure to ensure a separation between monetary policy and supervisory tasks. Whereas the Treaty on the Functioning of the EU establishes that the ECB is governed by the Governing Council, the SSM is de facto governed by a Supervisory Board. Decision-making within the SSM is based on a procedure known as "non-objection": if the ECB Governing Council does not object to a draft decision prepared by the Supervisory Board, the decision is deemed adopted.

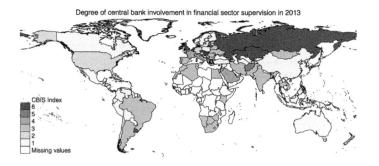

Degree of central bank involvement in financial sector supervision in 2013

CBIS Index
6
5
4
3
2
1
Missing values

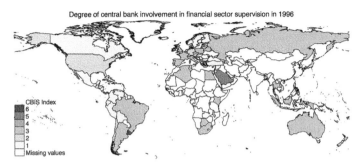

Degree of central bank involvement in financial sector supervision in 1996

CBIŞ Index
6
5
4
3
2
1
Missing values

Figure 3.1   Central bank involvement in financial supervision, 1996 and 2013

Source: Masciandaro and Romelli (2018).

What kind of measures are used under micro-prudential policy and supervision? To keep banks safe, they are required to comply with several regulatory ratios. These ratios aim to ensure that banks hold a minimum level of their own financial resources (i.e., *capital*) and a minimum level of liquid assets and stable funding (i.e., *liquidity*). The most important element of the regulatory framework consists of the minimum capital requirements for credit risk, as this is the main risk in banking. The Basel Committee on Banking Supervision (BCBS) establishes these rules at the global level. The BCBS is the primary global standard setter for the prudential regulation and supervision of banks, and provides an international forum for cooperation on banking supervisory matters. Its work led to several international agreements (see Box 3.1).

BOX 3.1   BASEL COMMITTEE ON BANKING SUPERVISION[4]

The BCBS provides a forum for regular cooperation on banking supervisory matters. Its objective is to improve the quality of banking supervision worldwide. Cooperation among supervisors was needed as competing regulatory standards from different jurisdictions endanger global financial stability and, in the end, would threaten the level playing field across regional markets.

The committee has developed supervisory standards, such as Basel I, Basel II and Basel III agreements. The Basel I Accord introduced a minimum regulatory capital constraint of 8 per cent, subject to a simple risk-weighting structure. The *risk-weighted capital requirement* specifies how much capital banks need to hold against risk-weighted assets (RWAs).

In 2004, an agreement was reached that is generally referred to as the Basel II Accord. It uses a three-pillar concept: (1) minimum capital requirements, (2) supervisory review, and (3) market discipline. Basel II aimed to align regulatory capital requirements more closely with the underlying risks that banks face. To calculate risk weights for each asset class, a standardized approach or internal models can be used (subject to supervisory approval). The standardized approach sets risk weights by exposure class. For example, for an exposure of €100, a risk weight of 50 per cent implies that the RWAs are €50. The industry had asked for a more refined approach towards risk-weighting, allowing for the use of banks' internal risk models.[5]

In response to the financial crisis, the BCBS made several changes in 2010, generally referred to as Basel III. This accord follows the three-pillar structure of Basel II: The first pillar covers the minimum capital requirements for credit risk, operational risk and market risk. The minimum capital requirements in the first pillar serve as a buffer against unexpected losses, thereby protecting depositors and the overall stability of the financial system. Basel III also introduced a minimum leverage ratio, i.e., the ratio between a bank's non-risk-weighted total exposures and its Tier 1 capital.[6] These exposures include total assets (on the bank's balance sheet), derivative exposures and securities financing transactions (both off balance sheet). Basel III also introduced liquidity requirements. Basel III established additional capital requirements for systemically important institutions. These are large, complex, interconnected financial institutions that may cause significant disruption to the wider financial system and economic activity if they fail.

The second pillar (supervisory review) requires supervisory authorities to examine the banks' activities and risk profiles to assess the need to hold additional capital (in addition to the level of capital calculated under the first pillar). The third pillar aims to enhance market discipline by increasing the transparency of the amount and composition of a bank's capital relative to its risk profile, thereby introducing incentives for banks to conduct their business in a safe, sound and efficient manner.

The negotiations about the final phase of Basel III were completed in December 2017. The final revision sought to restore the credibility of risk-weighted capital requirements by limiting the extent to which banks can rely on internal models. Importantly, it was agreed to limit the use of internal models: risk-weighted assets resulting from internal models cannot comprise less than 72.5 per cent of the risk-weighted assets deriving from the standardized approach. This so-called output floor will be phased in very gradually. The date for implementation was first scheduled for January 2022, with an additional five years of transitional period. However, the COVID-19 pandemic made the BCBS decide to push back the implementation date to the beginning of 2023, so 2028 is the final deadline.

3.3   MACRO-PRUDENTIAL SUPERVISION[7]

During and after the 2007/08 Global Financial Crisis (GFC), there has been a debate, both inside and outside central banks, about how to maintain financial stability (Blinder *et al.*, 2017). Two issues were key in this debate. First, which role should central banks have in maintaining financial stability? And second, should monetary policy be used for financial stability purposes? These issues will be discussed in turn in this section.

Before the GFC, the common view among central bankers was that achieving price stability would promote financial stability. Nowadays, in stark contrast, many central bankers see financial stability as an important objective in its own right. First, because the costs of financial crises are large (see below). Second, because financial stability is a precondition for price stability as acknowledged in many revised monetary policy strategies (see section 2.2). And third, because financial crises may affect the way monetary policy affects the economy, i.e., the so-called monetary transmission mechanism (as discussed in section 2.5).

One of the lessons learned as a consequence of the GFC is that sustained price stability does not automatically guarantee financial stability. Financial imbalances and vulnerabilities can build up under the calm surface of price stability. Indeed, price stability may have inadvertently contributed to risks of financial instability. The low volatility of both inflation and output fluctuations during the so-called Great Moderation (the decades before the financial crisis) may have lulled financial markets into thinking there was less risk in the economic system than was really the case. Some research suggests that benign economic environments may promote excessive risk-taking and may actually make the financial system more fragile (Mishkin, 2017).

Another lesson learned during the GFC is that the costs of cleaning up the damages caused by a financial crisis are very high. Financial crises are typically followed by prolonged periods of slow growth (Mishkin, 2017). For instance, Reinhart and Reinhart (2010) document that recessions following financial crises are more serious than normal recessions. These authors analyse 15 severe post-Second World War financial crises, as well as the Great Depression, the 1973 oil shock period and the GFC, and find that real GDP growth rates were significantly lower during the decade following each of these episodes, while unemployment rates stay persistently higher for a decade after crisis episodes. So, the cumulative output losses from financial crises are massive.

It is therefore not a surprise that central bankers have been allocated a key role in supporting financial stability with the conduct of macro-prudential policy. Cerutti *et al.* (2015) document the use of macro-prudential policies in a set of 119 countries over the 2000–2013 period. These authors show that the use of macro-prudential policies is widespread. However, emerging market economies (EMEs) tend to implement macro-prudential policies more related to foreign currency positions, while advanced economies (AEs) focus on borrower-based policies (such as loan-to-value and debt-to-income ratios).[8] This is confirmed by more recent BIS data as shown in Figure 3.2. Cerutti *et al.* (2015) also report that macro-prudential policies are generally associated with reductions in the growth rate in credit, but this effect is less evident in more developed and financially open economies.

Macro-prudential policy has two dimensions depending on the risk dimension focused upon: a "cyclical" dimension, which captures financial imbalances (like asset-price bubbles), and a "structural" dimension, which focuses on the interconnectedness of individual financial institutions and markets, as well as their common exposure to economic risk factors (Galati and Moessner, 2018). An example of a cyclical instrument is the *counter-cyclical capital buffer* (CCyB). The CCyB requires banks to increase their capital cushions during an economic expansion when

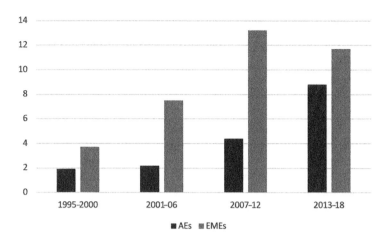

Figure 3.2   Use of macro-prudential policies, 1995–2018

Note: The bars show the average number of macroprudential measures per year and per 10 economies in each group of economies.
Source: Bank for International Settlements.

financial stability risks increase and then releases them in an economic downturn to absorb losses. Reducing requires capital when the economy slows, helps banks maintaining credit supply and avoids a drop in bank lending that would deepen the economic downturn. An illustrative example of a structural macro-prudential instrument is *loan-to-value (LTV) limits*. The LTV ratio expresses the value of a loan (e.g., a mortgage) to the value of an asset purchased (e.g., a house). Lowering the allowed LTV limit of residential mortgage loans will make the financial position of homeowners more resilient so that banks that provide these loans become less vulnerable.

Although central banks in many countries play an important role in or are responsible for macro-prudential policies, the governance of these policies differs a lot across countries. Most countries have a financial stability committee (FSC). Edge and Liang (2019, 2020) report that 47 out of the 58 countries in their dataset have such a committee, whereas before the crisis only 12 countries did. Most of these FSCs have three or four members, including the bank prudential regulator, the central bank, the ministry of finance and, when they are separate from the bank prudential regulator, securities regulators and other financial regulators. FSCs vary greatly in terms of responsibility for monitoring and identifying systemic risks and initiating or taking actions to reduce these risks. Only three FSCs (including France's High Council for Financial Stability and the UK's Financial Policy Committee) can directly implement countercyclical policies, while ten others can issue "comply or explain" directives, in which an agency is expected to respond by taking the directed action or explain why it did not. So, most FSCs are either advisory—with the ability to issue warnings and non-binding recommendations but without the ability to take or direct actions of the member agencies—or facilitate information sharing, communication and policy coordination across agencies. To illustrate this further, Table 3.1 shows which agency bears the ultimate responsibility for the instruments discussed earlier, i.e., the CCyB and LTV ratios.

Apart from the optimal involvement of central banks in macro-prudential policies, another important question that has been intensively discussed after the GFC is whether central banks should also employ monetary policy to maintain financial stability.[9] In particular, should they try to forego financial bubbles (often referred to as *"lean against the wind"*)? Before the GFC, many central banks thought they should take financial stability into account only if it affected the medium-term outlook for price stability. For example, the central bank should respond to asset price declines only after a bubble had burst. But several authors (e.g., Borio and

Table 3.1   Responsibility for macro-prudential tools

Country designates an authority:	CCyB	LTV
Yes	53	39
No	5	19
If Yes, which agency:		
FSC	3	2
Central bank	32	22
Ministry of Finance	3	7
Prudential regulator	16	7
Other	1	2

Source: Edge and Liang (2019)

White, 2004) argue that monetary policy should "lean against the wind", i.e., raise interest rates to prevent asset-price bubbles.

Opponents of leaning against bubbles raise three main objections. First, many observers doubt that financial imbalances can be identified with reasonable confidence in time to respond pre-emptively with monetary policy. Second, others doubt that monetary policy is the proper instrument to deal with financial imbalances like high debt levels. Svensson (2016), for example, argues that the effect of leaning against the wind may be small. Furthermore, even if tighter monetary policy rate slows down the growth rate of nominal debt, it also slows down the growth rate of nominal GDP. So, the debt-to-GDP ratio might even rise. In addition, the evidence suggests that interest rates would have to be raised substantially to curb risk-taking (Laeven, 2016). Finally, Svensson (2016) argues that the full costs of a crisis could be higher under a policy of leaning against the wind, because doing so will make the economy weaker before the crisis (higher interest rates will lead to lower growth).

Clearly, opinions differ widely over whether and how central banks should be responsible for financial stability. According to previous Fed Chair Janet Yellen (2014), "macro-prudential policies, such as regulatory limits on leverage and short-term funding, as well as stronger underwriting standards, represent far more direct and likely more effective methods to address these vulnerabilities" than monetary policy. In other words, yes, central banks ultimately carry a responsibility for financial stability, but monetary policy should not be the primary instrument.

3.4   CRISIS MANAGEMENT

Crises occur frequently. In the last two decades, several crises occured, like the Global Financial Crisis, the European sovereign debt crisis and, most recently, the crisis due to the COVID-19 pandemic. Central banks play a key role in crisis management. Crisis management has two aims (BIS, 2020). First, to prevent long-lasting damage to the economy by ensuring that the financial system continues to function and that credit to households and firms continues to flow. Second, to restore confidence and shore up private expenditures.

Central banks have several tools at their disposal for crisis management (BIS, 2020), of which a first set broadly aligns with the monetary policy tools discussed in sections 2.3 and 2.4. Typically, the first line of defence in crisis times is cutting short-term interest rates. By lowering the general cost of funds in the economy, policy rates have a wide reach. In addition, cutting rates sends a signal, which can help shore up confidence in times of stress. While interest rate cuts in crises are common, they are far from universal. In emerging market economies, stabilizing the exchange rate often requires raising interest rates to stem capital flight.

Second, central banks can lend to financial institutions. This includes open market operations and standing facilities but also targeted lending operations that can be tailored to support funding in specific market segments.

Third, central banks can employ outright asset purchases. Not only do asset purchases impact asset valuations, they also convey signals about the future course of policy and help manage expectations, thereby reducing uncertainty.

All these measures are part of the monetary policy toolkit of central banks. Therefore, central banks can only deploy them in crisis management situations to the extent that their use is consistent with the pursuit of their mandate. In many situations in which financial stability is at risk this is the case, which has also been acknowledged in recent monetary policy strategy reviews when central banks concluded that financial stability is a precondition for price stability (see section 2.2). However, the link between crisis management and the monetary policy objectives may not always be clear-cut, e.g., when a crisis is caused by underlying structural economic problems or debt sustainability issues in the financial sector or with governments (see Box 4.2). In these cases, the central bank may find itself confronted with the dilemma that it can only help in resolving a crisis while—temporarily—foregoing on the pursuit of its mandate.

Fourth, beyond monetary policy and as regulatory and supervisory agencies, central banks may adjust regulations that directly affect financial intermediaries and markets, such as capital and liquidity requirements. Whenever the central bank does not have control over these tools, they need to be deployed in coordination with the relevant authorities.

Finally, central banks may use communication to calm down financial markets and reassure the public that they are in control. Although words may be powerful in crisis times, they may often need to be backed up by deeds.

The important role of central banks in crisis management can be illustrated with the experiences during the three most recent crises: the GFC, the European sovereign debt crisis and the COVID-19 crisis. The three case studies are not an encompassing discussion of the respective crises, but rather serve as illustrations of how central banks have responded to crises originating from different sectors of the economy, respectively the financial sector, the government and the non-financial private sector (i.e., households and firms).

3.4.1   Crisis management by the Fed during the Global Financial Crisis

After several months of stirred market conditions, in the fall of 2008 a financial crisis impacting global financial markets and the global economy unfolded, originating from the financial sector in the US and triggered by the collapse of the investment bank Lehman Brothers. In the US, the Fed intervened on a grand scale using its powers under section 13(3) of the Federal Reserve Act, which gave the central bank virtually unlimited lending powers under "unusual and exigent circumstances" (under the Dodd–Frank Act, Congress limited that power).[10] Kohn (2010) provides a summary of the measures that the Fed implemented, including providing backstop liquidity to non-bank financial institutions on top of the traditional liquidity provision to banks and the purchase of large amounts of longer-term securities to ease financial conditions on top of lowering policy rates. According to Meltzer (2010: 1243),

> Never before had [the Federal Reserve] taken responsibility as lender-of-last-resort to the entire financial system, never before had it expanded its balance sheet by hundreds of billions of dollars or more over a short period, and never had it willingly purchased so many illiquid assets that it must hope will become liquid assets as the economy improves. Chairman Ben Bernanke seemed willing to sacrifice much of the independence that Paul Volcker restored in the 1980s. He worked closely with the Treasury and yielded to pressures from the chairs of the House and Senate Banking Committee and others in Congress.

As the crisis quickly spread to other parts of the world, many other central banks followed suit in terms of amending their policy tools to address the market turmoil and support the economy. Yet, since at the start of the crisis the US was the epicentre of the financial shock, no central bank innovated more dramatically at that stage than the Fed (Kohn, 2010).

3.4.2   Crisis management by the ECB during the euro area debt crisis

The second example refers to the euro area debt crisis. In 2009, the euro celebrated its tenth anniversary, yet a shock was unfolding in Greece that materialized into a full-blown financial crisis in subsequent months. After several revisions of previously announced deficit figures had been published, it became clear that public finances in Greece were unsustainable. The 10-year yield spread between Greek and German government bonds increased strongly, reaching about 1,000 basis points in May 2010. Similar concerns arose in Ireland, Portugal and, later, in Spain, Italy and Cyprus. Although the underlying cause of the crisis in some of these countries went beyond problematic public finances, the crisis did materialize with financial markets losing their confidence in public debt sustainability. Despite large-scale financial support from other euro area countries and the International Monetary Fund for countries hit by the crisis, turbulence at financial markets remained. Financial markets had started pricing currency convertibility risk into the government bonds of several stressed euro area countries reflecting a perceived risk that these countries could at some point be forced to leave the euro area and readopt a national currency. Traders and others started wondering explicitly whether these bonds would eventually be repaid in euros or in re-introduced national currencies. It was only after ECB President Mario Draghi told an investment conference in London in July 2012 that, "[w]ithin our mandate, the ECB is ready to do whatever it takes to preserve the euro. And believe me, it will be enough", that bond spreads of Greece, Ireland, Italy, Portugal, and Spain started to decline substantially.[11] To deliver on this commitment, the ECB introduced the Outright Monetary Transactions (OMT) programme in September 2012. Under this programme, the ECB can make purchases ("outright transactions") in secondary, sovereign bond markets, under certain conditions, of bonds issued by euro area member states. With this instrument, the ECB guaranteed the survival of the monetary union. President Draghi's unequivocal statement and the

Table 3.2   Central bank interventions in response to the COVID-19 crisis

Type of tool	Measure	Advanced economies							Emerging market economies							
		US	EU	JP	GB	CA	AU	CH	BR	CN	ID	IN	KR	MX	TH	ZA
Interest rate	Policy rate cut	x			x	x	x		x	x	x	x	x	x	x	x
Lending/ liquidity	Gen. liquidity provision	x	x	x	x	x	x		x	x	x	x	x	x	x	x
	Specialized lending	x	x	x	x				x	x	x	x	x	x	x	x
Asset purchases/ sales	Government bonds	x	x	x	x	x	x				x	x	x		x	x
	Commercial paper	x	x	x	x	x							x			
	Corporate bonds	x	x	x	x	x							x	x		
	Other private securities	x	x			x										
FX swap/ intervention	USD swap line	x	x	x	x	x	x	x					x	x		
	Interventions						x	x			x	x	x	x		
Prudential rules and regulation	Capital requirements	x	x	x	x	x	x	x	x	x	x	x	x	x		x
	Liquidity requirements	x	x	x	x	x	x	x	x	x	x	x	x	x	x	x
	Payout restrictions		x		x	x	x	x			x	x	x	x	x	x
	Market functioning	x	x	x	x	x	x	x	x	x	x	x	x	x	x	x

US=USA; EU=euro area; JP=Japan; GB=UK; CA=Canada; AU=Australia; CH=Switzerland; BR=Brazil; CN=China; ID=Indonesia; IN=India; KR=Korea; MX=Mexico; TH=Thailand; ZA=South Africa

Source: BIS (2020).

subsequent announcement of the ECB's OMT programme were sufficient to calm markets without spending a single euro under this programme.

3.4.3   Crisis management during the COVID-19 crisis

Finally, central banks played a very active role during the COVID-19 crisis, i.e., the economic crisis following the global pandemic that emerged as of early 2020. Table 3.2 illustrates that central banks all over the world took several measures to fight the crisis.

In contrast to the Global Financial Crisis, this crisis was at its core a shock to the economy generated by a health crisis and measures to address a public health emergency, constraining households and firms from engaging in economic activity. To contain the spread of the novel coronavirus, authorities shut down firms offering services that involve either large crowds or close human contact, such as entertainment, tourism, restaurants, retailing (other than necessities) and personal care. In addition, social distancing measures disrupted production in sectors that require a high degree of collective activity on-site, such as manufacturing and construction. As production in manufacturing is largely organized via global supply chains, production in many countries was severely hampered by disruptions elsewhere (BIS, 2020).

Different from the GFC, banks were not the source of the initial disturbance. Rather, they became involved as a consequence of the turmoil triggered by the economic contraction and because of a need to provide credit support to households and firms that were suddenly cut off from their regular sources of income. According to the BIS (2020: 38),

> central banks deployed their full array of tools and acted in their capacity as lenders of last resort—a function that has historically been at the core of their remit.[12] Apart from cutting interest rates swiftly and forcefully, down to the effective lower bound in a number of countries, central banks deployed their balance sheets extensively and on a very large scale. They injected vast amounts of liquidity into the financial system and committed even larger sums through various facilities. For instance, the Federal Reserve purchased over $1 trillion of government bonds in the span of about four weeks. This was roughly equal to the total amount of government bonds purchased under the large-scale asset purchase (LSAP) programmes between November 2008 and June 2011 …. Similarly, the ECB launched a facility to buy up to €1.35 trillion of securities, or around half of the total amount purchased under its Asset Purchase Programme between 2014 and 2018. In a matter of weeks, the balance sheets of the central banks of the major economies expanded substantially ….[13]

This is illustrated in Figure 3.3. The panel on the left shows balance sheet growth of the Federal Reserve, the ECB, the Bank of Japan, the Bank of

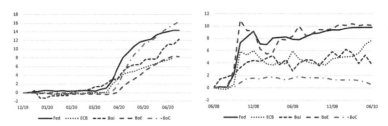

Figure 3.3   Balance sheet growth during the global financial crisis
and the COVID-19 crisis

Source: BIS (2020).

England and the Bank of Canada (BoC) during the COVID-19 crisis, while the panel on the right shows balance sheet growth of these central banks during the Global Financial Crisis. The figure illustrates that balance sheet growth during the COVID-19 crisis mostly exceeds balance sheet growth during the GFC.

In addition, central banks introduced supervisory measures aimed at supporting banks' ability and willingness to lend. For instance, capital requirements were temporarily relaxed. Central banks also restricted banks' dividend payments and buy-back activities. Paying dividends or buying own shares reduce the amount of capital available, and thus diminish banks' cushions to absorb losses and their ability to provide credit. For instance, the ECB issued a "recommendation" that supervised institutions would not pay out dividends for the financial years 2019 and 2020 and should refrain from buy-backs. This recommendation has expired on 30 September 2021.

Importantly, these central bank actions went hand in hand with large-scale fiscal policy support packages designed to cushion the blow to the real economy. As the BIS (2020: 23–24) points out, these fiscal policy measures were an important element of the overall crisis response:

> Crucial as they have been, central bank responses have a fundamental limitation. They provide temporary financing, but cannot transfer real resources. As such, they all generate additional debt and can only help borrowers survive if the income loss is not too large. For much the same reason, some borrowers run the risk of shifting the problems to the banking sector should that income loss become too large. This points to the dual importance of fiscal policy. First, it can act as a backstop to the extraordinary measures central banks have

taken. Governments can provide partial or complete indemnities to facilitate central banks' funding for less creditworthy firms. This can help to clarify the dividing line between monetary and fiscal policies as well as free central banks to concentrate on their mandate. Second, and more importantly, fiscal policy can transfer real resources to firms and households, to ease income shortfalls. This, of course, is in addition to the resources needed to directly tackle the health emergency in the first place.

Chapter 4 will discuss the relationship between monetary and fiscal policy in more detail.

NOTES

1. Their study also documents that countries are more likely to change their supervisory architecture when there are several other countries around the world or on the same continent undertaking reforms. The degree of central bank independence (CBI) also influences the decision to concentrate financial sector supervision in the hands of monetary policy authorities. Specifically, greater CBI is associated with less central bank involvement in supervision.
2. Banks had large exposures on governments, especially their own government. This led to the so-called *doom loop*: when a sovereign loses market access, as happened during the euro area sovereign debt crisis, the value of bank portfolios falls dramatically and banks need help from the government to stay solvent. This, in turn, increases borrowing pressure on the already stressed sovereign and further reduces the value of the bonds. Under those circumstances, governments are inclined to support and rescue banks in their jurisdiction, ignoring the interests of other countries.
3. However, the micro-prudential supervision of other financial intermediaries, such as insurance companies and pension funds, is still conducted outside the central bank.
4. This box draws on de Haan *et al.* (2020) and Enria (2021).
5. It is sometimes argued that this move towards the use of internal models in the calculation of capital requirements was at the origin of the Global Financial Crisis. According to some critics, relying on banks' own internally developed methodologies to calculate their regulatory requirements was like letting the fox guard the chicken coop. However, some of the jurisdictions at the epicentre of the crisis, such as the United States, had by then not allowed banks to use internal models (Enria, 2021).
6. Tier 1 capital consists of shareholders' equity and retained earnings.
7. This section heavily draws on Blinder *et al.* (2017) and de Haan *et al.* (2020).
8. Borrower-based instruments, like LTV limits, aim at mitigating the indebtedness of individuals or households. Lender-based macro-prudential instru-

ments, such as higher risk weights for mortgage-backed loans or limits on loan maturities, focus on the providers of loans.

9. This part heavily draws on Blinder *et al.* (2017).

10. Several institutions had an exposure on Lehman that became virtually worthless. For instance, the Reserve Primary Fund, one of the largest money market funds, owned $700 million of Lehman Brothers' short-term paper and came into serious financial difficulties due to its collapse. This, in turn, led to a flight to safety resulting in large-scale redemptions from prime US money market funds. The Fed and other central banks stepped in. Other financial institutions also needed support. For instance, the world's largest insurance company, American International Group, received an emergency loan in return for an 80 per cent public stake in the firm. The mortgage agencies Fannie Mae and Freddie Mac, accounting for nearly half of the outstanding mortgages in the US, were nationalized. The landscape of American finance radically changed. Bank of America bought investment bank Merrill Lynch. Two investment banks, Goldman Sachs and Morgan Stanley, converted themselves into commercial banks. In a rescue deal backed by US authorities, Washington Mutual and Wachovia were sold to JPMorgan Chase and Citigroup, respectively.

11. At https://www.ecb.europa.eu/press/key/date/2012/html/sp120726.en.html

12. A striking feature of the lender of last resort role of central banks during the COVID-19 crisis was the prevalence of interventions aimed at non-bank financial institutions, including entities such as money market funds. Similar to developments during the GFC, large-scale withdrawals had large knock-on effects on crucial funding markets, particularly on that for commercial paper, where prime money market funds are key investors. The Federal Reserve reacted swiftly, establishing a facility to backstop money market funds. This stemmed redemptions and averted a wider market breakdown (BIS, 2020).

13. In the euro area, the announcement of the Pandemic Emergency Purchase Programme (PEPP) helped narrow sovereign bond spreads, just as the announcement of Outright Monetary Transactions had back in 2012.

4. Challenges for central banks

4.1 LOW INTEREST ENVIRONMENT

Until very recently, both short-term and long-term nominal interest have been low for an extended period of time. As explained in section 2.3, if policy rates are at their effective lower bound, central banks may have to resort to unconventional monetary policies, such as asset purchase programmes and forward guidance, to counter risks to price stability. There is a debate, among both academics and policy-makers, about the causes of these low interest rates. Before summarizing the main issues in the debate it should be pointed out that, although nominal interest rates were for an extended period of time at historically low levels, real long-term interest rates—i.e., nominal long-term interest rates corrected for expected inflation that in most traditional economic models affect consumption spending and investment—have been negative in the past. Especially during periods of hyperinflation caused by wars or crises, real rates dropped to very low levels.[1] As a consequence, in historical perspective, current real long-term interest rates are not exceptionally low (Bonam *et al.*, 2018). The difference with past episodes of negative real rates is that in most recent years very low nominal interest rates are accompanied by an equally low inflation rate.

The discussion about low interest rates is generally framed in terms of the so-called *natural (or equilibrium or neutral) interest rate* r*. It is typically defined as the real rate of interest consistent with full employment and stable prices. In this sense, it can also be seen as the interest rate in the reaction function of central banks that prevails when there is no slack (i.e., the economy is operating at full capacity), and price stability is maintained (see Box 2.2). In the long run, the natural rate is determined by the supply of and demand for savings. The interest rate that equates supply and demand is the natural rate. Most evidence suggests that r* has declined during the last three decades (see, for instance, Holston *et al.*, 2017). But there is considerable uncertainty in these estimates.

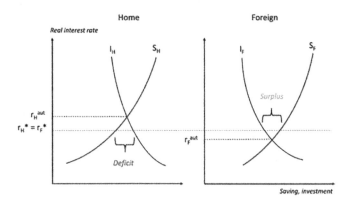

Figure 4.1   Global equilibrium real interest rate

Source: Obstfeld (2020).

With open capital markets, the natural rate is determined not at the national level but at the global level. Drawing on Obstfeld (2020), this can be explained using Figure 4.1. Suppose the world consists of two regions: Home and Foreign. In each region, saving increases with higher interest rates, while investment is decreasing with higher interest rates. This reflects that high interest rates will convince savers to save more, while low interest rates will incentivize borrowers to borrow. If both regions would have closed capital markets, the equilibrium rates would be r_H^{aut} and r_F^{aut}. These rates equate to domestic saving and investment. In an integrated world financial market, the real interest rates prevailing in Home (r_H^*) and Foreign (r_F^*) will be equalized by net international capital flows. In this equilibrium, Home's deficiency of saving compared with investment is offset by Foreign's excess of saving over investment.

Of course, Figure 4.1 is a very simplified model, but it enables discussing the main explanations for the decline in r*. There are several factors that can affect the supply of and demand for saving. One such factor is productivity growth. High productivity growth is generally associated with new investment opportunities for firms that increase the demand for capital, driving up interest rates. In recent years, productivity growth has been quite low, driving down the neutral rate.

But the saving schedule may also shift. One explanation for the decline of r* is the so-called *Global Savings Glut*. According to this view, the export-oriented policies of emerging market economies like China flooded capital markets with an increased supply of global savings in the early 2000s. This can be visualized in Figure 4.1 as an outward shift in the Foreign saving schedule, which lowers the world's natural rate of interest.

Another important reason for an increased supply of savings is demographic change. The share of people in the ages 40–64 in the world's total population increased to over 30 per cent by 2010, while it was around 25 per cent in the 1950s (Lundvall, 2020). A high proportion of middle-aged people leads to a high average saving ratio, as they all save for their pension.

Likewise, people may become more risk-averse and therefore increase their savings. People may also save more as a buffer against future uncertainty. This could increase demand for ultra-safe assets, like US Treasury bills or German bunds, which are very easy to buy and sell and have a very low default risk. Equally, central bank QE programmes increase the demand for safe assets and hence their scarcity.

What are the policy implications of a low natural interest rate? And what can monetary policy do? Two very different answers to these questions have been put forward. According to the secular stagnation hypothesis (Summers, 2014), the low natural rate of interest is an equilibrium phenomenon caused by various factors as discussed above, like a decline in population growth and a reduction in investment demand, which lead to a savings surplus. If r* is below the effective lower bound and inflation is below target, conventional monetary policy can no longer lower interest rates to the level required to stimulate private sector spending. However, fiscal policy can still help to stimulate demand, for example, through tax cuts and higher public spending.

By contrast, according to the financial cycle hypothesis, low interest rates are associated with financial booms and busts. Several countries had built up large financial imbalances before the Global Financial Crisis, and when these collapsed, this led to a deep worldwide recession. Central banks responded to this by cutting interest rates. Persistently low policy rates contributed to a reduction in r*, because accommodative monetary conditions encouraged a misallocation of production factors (by encouraging investments in less profitable sectors), which depresses economic growth. The low natural rate of interest is thus associated with the course of the financial cycle and is not an equilibrium phenomenon, as posited in the secular stagnation hypothesis (Borio *et al.*, 2017).

In theoretical models, the natural rate of interest plays an important role in monetary policy-making. Typically, inflation targeting central banks set the nominal policy interest rate less projected inflation above r* when inflation is expected to be above target, and below r* in the opposite case (Obstfeld, 2020). However, central bankers have stressed that because r* cannot be directly observed and estimates of r* are subject to uncertainty, monetary policy has to be cautious about using it as a benchmark in practice. For example, New York Fed President John Williams (2018b) downplays the use of the natural rate: "Back when interest rates were well below neutral, r* appropriately acted as a pole star for navigation. But, as we have gotten closer to the range of estimates of neutral, what appeared to be a bright point of light is really a fuzzy blur, reflecting the inherent uncertainty in measuring r*."

Still, low values of r* are likely to remain for some time, especially in the advanced economies, and different central banks have explicitly acknowledged this as a main structural characteristic of the macroeconomic environment in the years to come. All else equal, a lower r* implies that central banks will experience more frequently and more persistently that their policy rates will be at their effective lower bound than in the past. This also implies that central banks will need to use unconventional policies more often (see also section 2.2).

4.2   INFLATION PUZZLES AND MONETARY POLICY

With most central banks pursuing a low and stable rate of inflation as a primary policy objective, understanding the drivers of inflation is of crucial importance for monetary policy analysis and decision-making. However, this has proven more difficult in practice than textbook macroeconomic models on monetary policy would suggest. Central banks have imperfect knowledge about the drivers of inflation and imperfect control over inflation. They need to account for this in their monetary policy strategies. For example, because of the long and uncertain lags in the transmission mechanism of monetary policy, central banks do not target current inflation, but they typically target inflation over a flexible medium-term horizon.

This section discusses four apparent inflation puzzles that policy-makers and researchers have been confronted with in the last three decades (see Figures 4.2 and 4.3). The different periods can be considered as puzzles because there are several potential explanations that may have different implications for future inflation and monetary policy. To structure the discussion, we will look at the four puzzles through the lens of the Phillips curve (see Box 4.1).

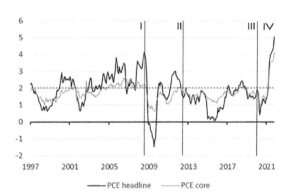

Figure 4.2   US PCE inflation: Year-on-year growth in PCE index

Note: I is the Great Moderation; II is the missing disinflation; III the missing reflation; and IV is the COVID-19 pandemic.

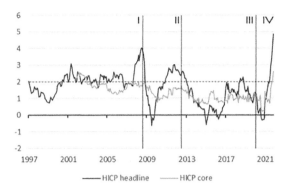

Figure 4.3   Euro area HICP inflation: Year-on-year growth in HICP
index

Note: I is the Great Moderation; II is the missing disinflation; III the missing
relfation; and IV is the COVID-19 pandemic.
Sources: FRED database and Eurostat.

BOX 4.1 INFLATION THROUGH THE LENS OF THE PHILLIPS CURVE

The analytical framework that links economic slack to wage and price
inflation and is a cornerstone of many macroeconomic models is known
as the Phillips curve. It is named after New Zealand economist A.W.
Phillips, who identified an inverse statistical relationship between unemployment and changes in wages in the UK in a seminal paper in 1958.
Since then, the Phillips curve has become known as the general framework for analysing the relationship between economic slack and wage
and price inflation. Intuitively, this can be explained as follows: A falling
unemployment rate signals an increase in the demand for labour, which
puts upward pressure on wages. If labour productivity growth is insuf-
ficient to compensate for higher wages, unit labour costs will increase,
driving up the production costs faced by firms. Profit-maximizing firms
will then try to pass on some or even all of these cost increases by raising
the prices of their products. This will lead to higher (actual and expected) inflation. For policy-makers, Phillips' findings suggested that there is
a policy trade-off between unemployment and inflation.

Over time, the Phillips curve framework has been updated and refined to account for advances in theoretical and empirical economic research. Notably, an apparent disappearance of a Phillips curve relationship in the data in the 1970s and the acknowledgment of the importance of incorporating expectations' formation in macroeconomic models implied a revolution in thinking about the relationship between slack and inflation. Specifically, it became conjectured that the traditional Phillips curve relationship only holds in the short term, because over the longer-term inflation expectations would adjust and the real economy would settle in its long-run equilibrium, which is determined by supply-side factors. Thus, an "expectations-augmented Phillips curve" implies that there may only be a trade-off between unemployment and inflation in the near term, i.e., until expectations adjust. Once expectations have adjusted in the long run, the Phillips curve is said to be vertical.[2]

4.2.1   The Great Moderation

After a decade of high inflation in the 1970s, inflation came down in the early 1980s ushering in an era that has become known as the Great Moderation, encompassing the 1990s and early 2000s. The Great Moderation was characterized by a period of low macroeconomic volatility, both in terms of output growth and inflation. Typically, the Great Moderation is not considered a puzzle, possibly because of its benign macroeconomic implications at the time. That being said, there is no consensus on the underlying causes of the Great Moderation and three potential, non-mutually exclusive explanations have been put forward (Bernanke, 2004).

A first explanation is that good policy was responsible for the Great Moderation. In particular, the increased independence of central banks pursuing clear and well-defined objectives ensured that monetary policy was credible and predictable, anchoring inflation expectations, which contributes to stable actual inflation and growth. In a Phillips curve context, well-anchored inflation expectations ensured that the little volatility in growth that did materialize, did not translate into large swings in inflation. In other words, anchored inflation expectations contributed to a relative flattening of the Phillips curve at the level of central banks' inflation targets.

A second explanation attributes the benign macroeconomic circumstances during the Great Moderation to good luck. This explanation conjectures that shocks hitting the economy were reduced in number and size during the Great Moderation. This is consistent with a reduction in the volatility of economic growth, which—even with an unchanged slope of the Phillips curve—also translates into less volatility in inflation. The good luck hypothesis suggests that swings in inflation would increase again as soon as the economy would become subject to larger shocks again.

Finally, a third explanation proposes that the Great Moderation was an outcome of structural changes in the economy. For example, a move from an economy based primarily on manufacturing to one in which services are more important, advances in information and communication technology, and more open trade and capital flows may have contributed to reduced macroeconomic volatility. All these factors may have made the economy more resilient to shocks, limiting volatility in economic activity and inflation. In particular, globalization has often been associated with a flattening of the Phillips curve, although empirical research remains inconclusive on its relative importance. Nevertheless, there is evidence of a global inflation cycle, suggesting that inflation is less responsive to domestic shocks (see section 4.3 for a more extensive discussion).

4.2.2   The missing disinflation in the Great Recession

The Great Moderation was forcefully interrupted by the Global Financial Crisis in late 2008 and early 2009, which led to a significant global downturn in economic activity currently known as the Great Recession. Triggered by the financial turmoil that originated in the US (see section 3.4.1), global economic activity dropped sharply, and unemployment increased. Considering that the slump in economic activity mostly constituted a shock to demand, slack in the economy also increased, which, in a Phillips curve framework, would be associated with a drop in inflation. As shown in Figures 4.2 and 4.3, headline inflation did indeed fall, even dipping into negative territory. However, this was mostly a consequence of a fall in energy prices. Indeed, as also shown in the graphs, the fall in underlying inflation—typically proxied by headline inflation excluding food and energy, or core inflation—fell by much less than anticipated based on Phillips curve analyses applied at the time.

Different explanations have been put forward for this period of apparent "missing disinflation". First, consistent with one of the explanations for the Great Moderation, it is argued that inflation did not fall as much as anticipated because of well-anchored inflation expectations. As the recession unfolded, anchoring kept the Phillips curve flat, insulating inflation from the global shock to economic activity. Similarly, the explanation for the Great Moderation that attributes a flattening of the Phillips curve to structural changes in the economy can also explain the missing disinflation after the Great Recession. Daly *et al.* (2012) argue, instead, that the impact of the recession on inflation was relatively muted because of downward wage rigidities. In other words, these authors suggest that the Phillips curve has not flattened in general but is only flat when economic conditions are relatively poor. By contrast, Coibion and Gorodnichenko (2015) argue that there was a negative impact of the recession on inflation consistent with the Phillips curve, but only when also accounting for the observation that household inflation expectations had increased at the onset of the crisis, which countered the downward impact of the recession on inflation.

Several authors have connected the missing disinflation to factors specific to the Global Financial Crisis and have argued that the Phillips curve framework needs to be expanded with financial factors. For example, Christiano *et al.* (2015) pose that increasing interest rate spreads during the crisis increased price pressures by increasing costs that firms face. Gilchrist *et al.* (2015) suggest that firms can raise prices when they face liquidity constraints. Both mechanisms would counter the disinflationary effect of a recession that is consistent with a Phillips curve.

4.2.3   The missing reflation: Persistently low inflation

When economies ultimately recovered from the Great Recession, instead of moving up, inflation trended down and stayed persistently below central banks' targets in many advanced economies, in particular in the euro area (see Figure 4.3). In other words, where disinflation was missing during the recession, reflation was missing during the recovery in spite of substantial monetary policy accommodation provided by central banks with both conventional and unconventional instruments (see section 2.3). Some of the potential explanations for the missing disinflation during the Great Recession are the mirror image of the explanations for the missing reflation during the recovery, specifically those explanations that relate to a general flattening of the Phillips curve. However, several alternative hypotheses have been proposed to explain persistently low inflation without a flattening of the Phillips curve.

Specifically, empirical research that takes a longer-term perspective has generally found that trend inflation has declined over time. Once accounting for this trend, several studies find that a Phillips curve relationship between economic slack and inflation can still be found around this declining trend (see e.g., Hindrayanto et al., 2019). These studies are typically more statistical in nature, i.e., they analyse the time-series properties of inflation while remaining silent about what the potential explanations could be for the declining trend in inflation. However, Bonam et al. (2019) present a review of the literature that suggests that contributing factors could be an ongoing globalization trend, the declining bargaining power of labour, demographic changes, technological progress and the rise of e-commerce, and financial factors.

An alternative explanation for the downward trend in inflation and, thus, the missing reflation is that inflation expectations had become unanchored, or—potentially equally problematic for monetary policy—that expectations had become anchored at a level below central banks' objective. Evidence for this hypothesis for the euro area is provided by Corsello et al. (2021), who find that long-term inflation expectations declined since 2014. Likewise, Ciccarelli and Osbat (2017) present evidence in support of the hypothesis that long-term inflation expectations in the euro area have become more dependent on current inflation, an indication of unanchored inflation expectations. However, their evidence for a de-anchoring of inflation expectations becomes weaker, the longer the horizon of expectations, suggesting that confidence in the ECB's commitment to its target had remained largely intact.

A final explanation for the missing reflation proposes that economic slack is estimated incorrectly in Phillips curve analyses. For example, when studying the wage Phillips curve, Bonam et al. (2021a) find that existing measures for the unemployment gap fail to adequately capture labour demand conditions. When using a novel measure for labour market slack based on a survey among firms—identifying hidden slack in the economy—the irresponsiveness of wage inflation to slack disappears, although there remains some evidence that the slope of the Phillips curve may have changed over time.

4.2.4   Quo vadis? Inflation after the COVID-19 pandemic

The COVID-19 pandemic represented an unprecedent shock to the global economy, in terms of both its size and how the shock transmits through the global economy (see, e.g., Baqaee and Fahri, 2020). For monetary policy, a key question is to what extent a pandemic materializes as a demand shock versus a supply shock. In the former case, a reduction in economic activity is associated with increased slack in the economy reducing inflation in accordance with the Phillips curve. In the latter case, supply-side factors reduce potential economic activity, which reduces economic slack and—again in line with the Phillips curve—increases inflationary pressures.

Intuitively, a pandemic can be considered to cause a mix of both effects. First, due to increased uncertainty about the consequences of the health crisis—both related to personal health and the economic outlook—it is likely that households reduce spending, which depresses demand. This is aggravated by containment measures that restrict possibilities for consumers to spend, in particular in specific service sectors like entertainment and hospitalities. At the same time, the pandemic also creates supply-side impediments. For example, labour input and pro-ductivity may be constrained because the workforce is restricted to come to the workplace, either due to the health impact of the pandemic or as a consequence of containment measures. Moreover, even if only a small number of firms is constrained by the direct effects of the pandemic, if these firms are part of a broader supply chain they may cause disruptions for production processes of many other firms in their supply chain. In an environment in which many supply chains are global in nature, this can become exacerbated when the pandemic leads to restrictions in interna-tional travel and trade as was the case during the COVID-19 pandemic. Finally, both the negative demand and negative supply-side dynamics can become amplified by financial factors if the pandemic causes disruptions in financial markets and risks for financial stability (see section 3.4.3 on how central banks managed these effects of the COVID-19 pandemic).

Ultimately, the relative importance of demand-side versus supply-side consequences depends on many factors, including the persistence of the pandemic, the way that the economy adapts to the pandemic, the policy response, and the conditions that prevail when the economy exits the pandemic. As a consequence, the relative importance of demand-versus supply side effects can differ across sectors and can change over time. Figures 4.2 and 4.3 show that at the onset of the pandemic inflation dropped sharply, suggesting that on aggregate negative demand consequences of the pandemic dominated. However, as of the second half of 2021 inflation has increased sharply, suggesting that supply-side constraints have gained in prominence relative to constraints to demand. Or, equivalently, the recovery in aggregate demand has been outpacing the recovery in aggregate supply. More recently, pandemic induced bottlenecks in supply chains and rising energy prices have become compounded by the Russian invasion of Ukraine, leading to inflation rates well above inflation targets in several advanced economies. In response, central banks terminated their asset purchase programmes and have started raising their policy rates.

Taking a longer-term perspective, Bonam and Smadu (2021) find that historically pandemics had a long-lasting downward impact on inflation, suggesting depressed demand for an extended period of time. At the same time, the authors acknowledge that it remains too early to tell whether this will be the same for the present pandemic, considering the unprecedented policy response to support demand and the prompt availability of vaccines that were absent in earlier pandemics.

4.2.5 Policy conclusions

The four puzzles presented underline the difficulty of analysing the underlying drivers of inflation, which complicates the assessment of the optimal policy response. If the Phillips curve has flattened and inflation expectations are well anchored at target, as has been suggested to be the case during the Great Moderation and the period of missing disinflation, central bankers can be relatively comfortable that inflation will be relatively resilient to shocks to the economy. If, however, the Phillips curve is flat and inflation expectations are not well anchored at target, central banks will have to adjust policy relatively forcefully to ensure a prompt reversal of deviations of inflation from target once they occur. Alternatively, if inflation dynamics are predominantly associated with structural or financial factors, or good (or bad) luck, central banks will have to assess to what extent these factors are expected to prevail in the future and warrant a monetary policy response.

In case of the current shock caused by the COVID-19 pandemic, central banks need to reassess on an ongoing basis how the relative demand- and supply-side consequences of the shock are expected to materialize in the future. Moreover, after a long spell of relatively low inflation before the pandemic, the recent increase in inflation may create risks of inflation expectations becoming unanchored above target, especially if the spell of high inflation turns out to be more persistent than most central banks initially anticipated. Finally, as the economy is adjusting and adapting to the COVID-19 shock, the underlying structural characteristics of the economy may change, which could also change the parameters of the Phillips curve linking economic activity and inflation.

4.3   EXTERNAL INFLUENCE ON MONETARY POLICY

One often mentioned potential explanation for the decades of low inflation until the pandemic discussed in section 4.2 was globalization. This section takes a deeper dive in the impact of external (i.e., foreign) factors on monetary policy by looking at the impact of external factors on inflation and on financial conditions.

4.3.1   Less impact of monetary policy on inflation due to globalization?

The growing integration of markets across different economies may be a factor contributing to a flattening of the Phillips curve. Kamber *et al.* (2020) note two key channels through which globalization can affect the slope of the Phillips curve. The first channel is greater foreign competition, which prevents firms from raising prices, even if the domestic economic situation would suggest they should. The second channel is the increased integration of emerging market economies into the global economy. Think about outsourcing of production to countries with lower wages. This not only puts downward pressures on wages in many sectors but may also reduce the bargaining power of workers, dampening the response of wages and prices to domestic economic slack. Despite extensive research, there is no consensus in the literature that globalization has flattened the Phillips curve (Obstfeld, 2020; Kamber *et al.*, 2020). Nevertheless, there is evidence suggesting that countries' inflation rates, at least to some extent, move in tandem (see Box 4.2).

BOX 4.2   GLOBAL INFLATION CYCLE

In the early 1970s, inflation surged worldwide. The fact that high inflation could transmit so easily globally was driven by the Bretton Woods system, under which all countries pegged to the US dollar (thereby surrendering monetary autonomy). Monetary policy in the US led to inflation, on top of which came the oil price hike. Since then, inflation has fallen around the world, with median annual global consumer price inflation down from a peak of 16.6 per cent in 1974 to 2.6 per cent in 2017 (Ha *et al.*, 2019). The decline began in advanced economies in the mid-1980s and in emerging market and developing economies in the mid-1990s. The similarity in inflation patterns has led to research on the so-called *global inflation cycle*. This is the notion that inflation is becoming less responsive to domestic economic conditions, and is instead increasingly determined by global factors that affect inflation in all countries. A strengthening global inflation cycle raises concerns that central banks' control over domestic inflation may have weakened. Former Bank of England governor Mark Carney (2015) wondered: "In this era of hyper-globalisation, are central banks still masters of their domestic monetary destinies? Or have they become slaves to global factors? …. There's evidence of global inflationary cycles that correspond with an intensifying globalisation that propagates common shocks via commodity, trade and financial channels."

The notion of a global inflation cycle is often analysed by estimating the extent to which inflation in different countries can be explained a single common factor (Kamber *et al.*, 2020). Research by Forbes (2019) indicates that over the last 25 years the shared global component of CPI inflation has more than doubled (from 27 per cent in 1990–94 to almost 57 per cent in 2015–17), while the findings of Ha *et al.* (2019) suggest that this common component can explain a high share of variance of inflation (in the order of 45–50 per cent). According to these authors, the emergence of a global inflation cycle was likely driven by multiple forces, including a variety of global shocks. In the median country, three global shocks—global demand shocks, global supply shocks and oil price shocks—have accounted for about one-quarter of domestic inflation variation since the 1970s, even though the importance of global shocks for domestic inflation was larger for advanced economies than for emerging and developing economies. Since 2001, the relevance of global shocks has increased accounting for more than half of the source of inflation variation in advanced economies. Of these, the most important were global demand (especially the Great Recession) and oil price shocks (especially the plunge of 2014–16). This is in line with the findings of Jašová *et al.* (2018) that the relevance of the global output gap for explaining domestic inflation in a Phillips curve framework has increased relative to the domestic output gap.

Although it is not clear that globalization has affected the slope of the Phillips curve, it is likely that globalization plays an important role in explaining the downward trend of inflation of the last decades. For instance, the relocation of production to the most cost-efficient firms typically leads to a decline of the prices of goods that have been outsourced. Likewise, organizing production through so-called production chains, i.e., to produce the several components needed to produce a good at different places in the world (think mobile phones), makes those goods cheaper. As such goods prices are a component of consumer prices, their fall has, to some extent, contributed to low overall inflation. In addition to such direct effects, increased competition may also have indirect effects by moderating domestic producer prices, as pointed out before.

Goodhart and Pradhan (2020) stress one dimension of globalization in explaining inflation dynamics, namely the rise of the economic importance of China. Its working population has become increasingly incorporated into the world's trading system. Together with the incorporation of Eastern Europe into the available world working force, and improved demography, the effective world's working age population more than doubled over the 30 years from 1980 to 2010. This led to a shift of production of tradeable goods and services from the high labour-cost areas in the West to the low labour-cost areas in the East. The result was a sharp rise in the wages in the East and relative stagnation in the wages in the West. Another important factor is the aging of the population in China as well as in almost every advanced economy, which made the proportion of young in the population decline sharply over the years 1970–2010. The falling ratio of dependents to workers is of, and by, itself disinflationary. As the authors explain: "In extremely simple terms, workers must produce goods and services of more value than their wages; otherwise it would not be economical to hire them. By the same token, the young and old, who are not working, consume, but do not produce. Therefore, they increase demand relative to supply." Goodhart and Pradhan (2020) point out that the dependency ratios are now reversing sharply in most countries. They expect that, once the COVID-19 pandemic is firmly behind us, inflation will recur. So, central banks would, under normal circumstances, raise their interest rates. But there is a problem: "This is that debt ratios, both in the public and private sectors, in most countries are so high that any significant rise in nominal interest rates would likely tip those economies back into recession, which would make everything worse. ... Concerns about the effects of rising interest rates under such conditions will lead to political pressures on central banks to allow inflation significantly in excess of present target levels." In other words, these countries are at risk of becoming subject to a regime of fiscal dominance (see section 4.4 and Box 4.5).

4.3.2   Impact of the global financial cycle

The possibilities for countries to pursue monetary policy aimed at price stability and stabilization independent of what happens in other countries are limited. According to the *Mundell–Fleming Trilemma*, only two of the following three factors are compatible: exchange rate stability, open capital markets and domestic monetary autonomy (see Figure 4.4). Under a fixed exchange rate regime, the scope for autonomous monetary policy is limited in the absence of capital restrictions. If investors can move money from one country to another (open capital markets), and they believe that the price of one currency for another will remain constant over time (fixed exchange rates), then an equal interest rate in both countries is the only way to achieve currency market equilibrium. Thus, countries cannot simultaneously conduct their own monetary policy, maintain a fixed exchange rate, and have free movement of capital.

Under the Gold Standard, the monetary trilemma was resolved in favour of exchange rate stability and freedom of foreign transactions. Under the Bretton Woods system, exchange rates were fixed while deviations from capital mobility, to greater or lesser extent, gave national authorities scope to manage domestic interest rates notwithstanding fixed exchange rates (Obstfeld and Taylor, 2017). However, over time, capital mobility increased and so did exchange rate flexibility. As shown in Figure 4.5, the level of capital mobility rose dramatically into the early 2000s, before levelling off and even declining during the last decade. The share of countries with pegged exchange rates fell dramatically from about 90 per cent in 1970 to about 40 per cent by the 1980s. But since then, the share of countries with pegged currencies has increased to more than half (Obstfeld and Taylor, 2017).

Figure 4.4   The Mundell–Fleming Trilemma

Source: Adrian (2018).

So, in the context of the monetary trilemma, many countries sacrificed fixed exchange rates in order to allow both international capital mobility and a monetary policy geared towards domestic objectives. According to the trilemma, under flexible exchange rates and capital mobility, a country would have more policy autonomy than under fixed exchange rates. However, recent literature suggests that the monetary policy auton-

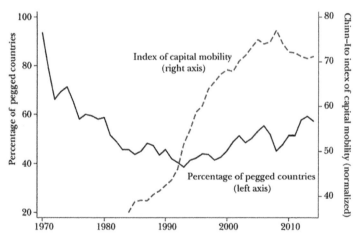

Figure 4.5   Capital mobility and fixed exchange rates in the world

Note: Capital account openness is measured using the (normalized) index developed by Chinn and Ito (2006).
Source: Obstfeld and Taylor (2017).

omy in a system of flexible exchange rates is also limited. Rey (2013) argues that even countries with flexible exchange rates do not have an independent monetary policy, as there is a global financial cycle, which is mainly determined by monetary policy in industrialized countries, in particular the US, and global risk aversion. Global financial cycles are associated with surges and retrenchments in capital flows, booms and busts in asset prices and crises, and are characterized by large common movements in asset prices and capital flows. Once the capital account is open, a global cycle would largely determine domestic financial conditions, i.e., the interest rates that non-financial corporates and households have to pay, irrespective of the ability of the domestic central bank to set the policy rate autonomously and the prevailing exchange rate regime. In other words, the choice of the exchange rate regime is virtually irrelevant. There is no longer a trilemma (according to which only two of the three objectives, i.e., fixed exchange rate, autonomous monetary policy and free movement of capital, can be achieved simultaneously), but a *dilemma*: a choice between autonomous monetary policy or capital mobility. Regardless of the exchange rate regime, monetary policy autonomy can only be achieved by delinking domestic financial conditions from the global environment through restrictions on international financial transactions.

According to research by Miranda-Agrippino and Rey (2020), the global financial cycle is driven mainly by US monetary policy and global risk aversion.[3] Drawing on Habib and Venditti (2018), Figure 4.6 depicts the complexity of the mechanisms. For instance, the stance of US monetary policy may affect risk attitude globally, but the causality may also run in the opposite direction. Monetary policy tightening that surprises markets is normally associated with an increase in risk aversion. At the same time, changes in risk aversion may induce changes in the stance of monetary policy to counteract the effects of these shocks on the economy.

Others disagree. For instance, Cerutti *et al.* (2017) challenge the view of Rey and her co-authors on empirical grounds. As explained by Rose (2017): "Despite the impression given by recent studies, most variation in capital flows for small and emerging markets has not been driven by the global financial cycle. No more than 25 per cent of the fluctuations in capital flows can be ascribed to fluctuations in global risk aversion or the stance of US monetary policy. This should be welcome news to policy-makers in small countries. On the other hand, it also means they

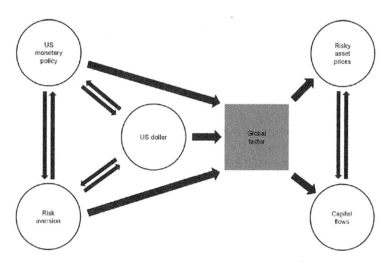

Figure 4.6   The drivers of the global financial cycle

Source: Habib and Venditti (2018).

cannot reasonably blame foreign influences for their domestic problems. Autonomy comes with responsibility." Likewise, Habib and Venditti (2018) challenge the view of a global financial cycle,

> that manifests itself through the co-movement of cross-border flows and translates into more aligned risky asset prices and external finance premia across different economies. This was the case in the run-up to the global financial crisis and in its aftermath, in particular for cross-border banking flows among advanced economies and for stock prices. However, after the crisis, the synchronization of capital flows and stock prices has abated, returning to the levels observed between the 1990s and the 2000s.

According to Obstfeld (2015), the trilemma still applies, even though financial globalization complicates monetary policy. When faced with external shocks, countries with floating exchange rates still have a shock absorber that countries that peg exchange rates lack and thus can achieve preferred policy outcomes even if they cannot fully insulate their economies. In this sense, more flexible exchange rates do provide a degree of insulation from external monetary shocks, as the trilemma predicts. But the absence of full isolation implies that monetary policy elsewhere, notably in the US, affects other countries, also those with a flexible exchange rate regime.

A well-known example of how Fed policies can result in large swings in global financial markets is the so-called *taper tantrum* episode of May 2013. In his testimony in the US Congress, then-chairman Bernanke hinted that the Fed would start scaling back its large-scale asset purchase programme. As a result, US yields surged, which triggered a sell-off in emerging markets. Another bout of capital outflows from emerging markets occurred in May 2018, when the Fed started to reduce its holdings of assets acquired under earlier programmes of quantitative easing (until then all maturing assets had been reinvested to maintain an equal size of its QE portfolios). This tapering, which was followed by a sell-off in US bond markets and an appreciation of the dollar, was halted in 2019. The reverse had happened earlier when US interest rates were low, causing huge capital inflows to emerging markets. Loose US monetary policies made investors seek higher yields in emerging markets. Box 4.3 provides an example how this works out in an emerging market economy.

BOX 4.3 HOW US MONETARY POLICY AFFECTS THE INDIAN ECONOMY

Apart from its impact on capital flows, US monetary policy also affects the exchange rate of the US dollar. This affects many emerging market economies (EMEs) as they have a high share of their debt denominated in dollars. A depreciation of the national currency (an appreciation of the dollar) deteriorates the balance sheets of non-financial and financial enterprises. This is because debt contracts are often denominated in dollars, which increases the debt burden in the event of a depreciation of the national currency, while there is no simultaneous increase in the value of assets, as they are usually denominated in domestic currency. Under these conditions, a local currency depreciation against the dollar can lower output by causing a deterioration in the balance sheet conditions of firms exposed to unhedged dollar debt. Firms' investment drops in response to a depreciation given firms' reduced ability to support credit in view of their weakened balance sheets.

Banerjee and Mohanty (2021) examine this using Indian firm-level data. India provides an example of a typical EME that relies heavily on foreign currency debt to finance domestic investment. The authors find that a tighter US monetary policy has an adverse effect on the financing conditions of Indian non-financial firms. Rupee depreciation combined with higher US interest rates and unhedged foreign currency debt precipitate a contraction in credit. Rupee depreciation magnifies liabilities that are valued in dollars and leads to a decline in the net worth of the borrowing firms. Indian domestic credit and business cycles go through a pronounced downswing for nearly six to eight quarters following the US monetary tightening. A 1 per cent hike in the Fed funds rate can depress domestic output in India by 0.76 per cent from their respective long-run levels.

4.4   COORDINATION WITH FISCAL POLICY[4]

In discussing how monetary and *fiscal policy*, i.e., policies regarding government spending and taxes, should be coordinated, a distinction can be made between normal and crisis times.

Under normal circumstances, monetary policy aims at price stability and (to the extent that it is not detrimental to price stability) at stabilization of the business cycle. A policy stance that tends to stabilize the business cycle is said to be countercyclical; otherwise, it is either neutral (i.e., no systematic impact on the cyclicality of economic activity) or procyclical (i.e., it tends to amplify fluctuations). In principle, fiscal policy can also be used for stabilization purposes. If the economy is in a recession, say, the government may increase spending and/or lower taxes and finance its revenues shortfall by issuing government debt. This expansionary policy will stimulate the economy, just like a cut in interest rates would. Likewise, during an economic boom, the government may decide to increase taxes to reduce government debt (contractionary fiscal policy).

However, there are three key differences between fiscal and monetary policy. First, the transmission of fiscal policy operates more directly, impinging on households' incomes and firms' profitability, while monetary policy works indirectly by changing the price and availability of credit. Second, monetary policy decisions and their implementation take less time than fiscal policy decisions and their implementation. This reflects that the government needs parliamentary approval to change spending or taxes and this process takes time (the legislative lag). Moreover, once a fiscal policy bill is accepted by parliament, it takes time to implement it (the implementation lag). Finally, it takes time for fiscal policy to have effect (the impact lag). These long lags make discretionary fiscal policy a less effective stabilization tool than monetary policy.[5] Third, politicians tend to prefer expansionary fiscal policy over contractionary policy. Notably during economic good times, they prefer not to increase taxes and limit spending. As a consequence, fiscal policies are often pro-cyclical, especially in good times (Alesina *et al.*, 2008). To mitigate these concerns with discretionary fiscal policies and in an attempt to add to the countercyclicality of overall fiscal policy, governments typically design "*automatic stabilizers*" in their fiscal framework, i.e., mechanisms that automatically loosen the fiscal stance when the economy slows down and that tighten the fiscal stance when the economy is booming (e.g., a progressive income tax system or unemployment benefits). Still, as central banks are (at least to some extent) insulated from the political process (see section 1.3), they are typically more willing than fiscal policy authorities to use contractionary policy when the economy is booming and inflation threatens to increase.

BOX 4.4 THE FISCAL POLICY MULTIPLIER

A key metric for fiscal policy effectiveness is the *fiscal multiplier* (i.e., the impact on GDP of a one unit increase in the government deficit). There is a large literature estimating fiscal multipliers (see Bonam *et al.*, 2021b for a discussion of the literature). Research suggests that multipliers depend on several factors. First, the literature suggests a reduced effect of fiscal policy when sovereign debt levels are already high. Expectations of sustained deficits leading to higher public debt may undermine investors' confidence in government's ability to face its obligations in full and in all circumstances. Second, multipliers tend to be higher when the interest rate is at its effective lower bound. Finally, there is evidence that the size of the multiplier also depends on the composition of government spending.

For a sample of 17 advanced economies, covering the 1960Q1–2017Q4 period, Bonam *et al.* (2021b) find that both the government consumption and investment multipliers are significantly higher, and exceed unity, when interest rates are persistently low. The government consumption multiplier peaks at around 2 at the ELB and 0.4 in normal times. For the government investment multiplier, the corresponding numbers are 1.2 and 0.8. Moreover, these authors find that the longer the spell that policy rates are at the ELB, the higher the multiplier.

Even though it is not optimal from a business cycle stabilization perspective, there are circumstances when monetary policy could add to procyclicality of economic activity. For instance, under forward guidance monetary authorities commit maintaining a relatively loose stance for a protracted period, even if economic conditions start improving (see section 2.4). If inflation continues to deviate persistently from target even when the economy is running at full capacity, keeping interest rates low in line with the forward guidance commitment can imply that the monetary stance becomes intentionally neutral or even procyclical.

An issue that is hotly debated in policy and academic circles alike is the optimal calibration of the *macroeconomic policy mix*, i.e., the combination of the stance of fiscal and monetary policy in relation to the economic outlook. There are three broad types of policy mix. First, both policies have a countercyclical stance. Following Bartsch *et al.* (2020), this is called a congruent mix. Second, when both policies are procyclical, the mix is destabilizing. Finally, when fiscal and monetary policy go in different directions, i.e., one is procyclical and the other is countercyclical, the mix is divergent.

As pointed out by Bartsch *et al.* (2020), a divergent policy mix may overburden one policy area with the task of delivering the appropriate countercyclical stance, responding to both the business cycle and the procyclical stance of the other policy area. For instance, if inflation is below target while fiscal policy is restrictive, the central bank has to take more action to raise inflation than if fiscal policy would be accommodative. This holds even more when the interest rate is at its effective lower bound, because conventional monetary policy (i.e., lowering policy interest rates) can then not be used. A divergent mix may also generate imbalances that erode both fiscal and/or monetary policy space, limiting the overall stabilization capacity of macroeconomic policy. For instance, if government debt increases due to expansionary fiscal policy while the central bank raises interest rates, the government has to pay a higher interest rate on its outstanding debt, thereby limiting the fiscal policy space.

Looking at data for 22 OECD countries over the period 1986–2019, Bartsch *et al.* (2020) conclude that a congruent policy mix is rarely achieved. The main culprit is a strong tendency for fiscal policy to be procyclical. Except during the GFC and during the 2002 slowdown, only a minority of countries managed to exhibit a congruent policy mix.

Looking at the evidence across countries confirms that congruence is a relatively rare event for most countries (see Figure 4.7). It is slightly

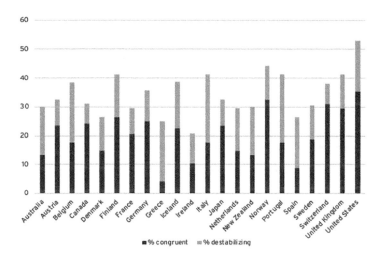

Figure 4.7   Share of congruent and destabilizing years (per cent)

Source: Bartsch *et al.* (2020).

more frequent in Switzerland, the United Kingdom, the United States, Norway, Finland and Germany. The policy mix is even more frequently destabilizing than congruent in Australia, Belgium, Greece, Italy, New Zealand, Portugal and Spain.

Figure 4.8 depicts how often the policy mix is divergent. Switzerland, Japan and the United Kingdom exhibit the lowest rates of policy divergence. Figure 4.8 shows that this divergence is more often due to a procyclical fiscal policy than to a procyclical monetary policy.

In crisis situations, like the COVID-19 crisis, policy-makers have no alternative but to massively deploy all instruments at their disposal. Indeed, as discussed in section 3.4, in response to the COVID-19 pandemic, policy-makers around the world quickly activated a broad range

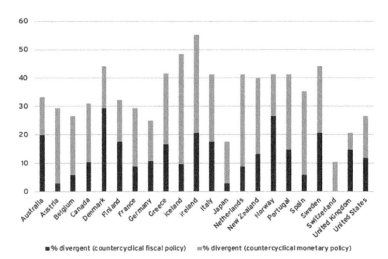

Figure 4.8   Share of years with divergent policy mix (per cent)

Source: Bartsch *et al.* (2020).

of fiscal and monetary policy instruments to provide exceptional support to counter the recession caused by the spread of the virus and lockdowns and social distancing measures. In this case, the policy mix was highly congruent in many economies.

Bartsch *et al.* (2020) point out that an appropriate mix of expansionary monetary and fiscal policies during a crisis creates policy space. The central bank creates fiscal policy space by (1) substantially lowering government's borrowing costs and (2) by effectively providing what is called a (perceived) monetary backstop to government debt. This means that the central bank commits to forego self-fulfilling sovereign debt crises, like the ECB did when it introduced OMT after ECB President Mario Draghi's "whatever it takes" speech. Likewise, the government creates monetary policy space by "backstopping" monetary authorities, i.e., guaranteeing to provide additional capital to the central bank when it incurs large portfolio losses from its monetary policy operations. Such insurance thus preserves the central bank's independence and credibility by enabling the significant risk-taking inherent to unconventional monetary operations.

However, these backstops are not without risks. Fiscal policy authorities may delay fiscal adjustments after the crisis is over to the point of undermining the credibility of the fiscal backstop. Similarly, for monetary policy authorities, there is a point beyond which stretching their balance sheet could undermine their credibility, resulting in unanchored inflation expectations and an inability to control aggregate financing conditions in the economy. In fact, several observers have expressed concerns that the policy mix pursued to counter the impact of the COVID-19 pandemic with highly accommodative monetary and fiscal policy may lead to what is called *fiscal dominance*, i.e., a situation where monetary policy is determined by the fiscal position of the government and is no longer directed at maintaining price stability (see Box 4.5).

BOX 4.5 THE RISK OF FISCAL DOMINANCE

Monetary policy cannot be credible and deliver price stability if the central bank becomes responsible for stabilizing public debt dynamics. A regime where public debt dynamics are stable so that monetary policy can keep inflation in check is often labelled as *monetary dominance*. Several observers have expressed worries that, due to the high level of government debt in most advanced economies, this monetary dominance regime may be replaced by a fiscal dominance regime. Rising indebtedness implies that governments will need to roll over increasing amounts of debt,[6] on top of the need to finance newly issued debt. According to ECB Executive Board member Isabel Schnabel (2020), "some observers have taken the launch of the asset purchase programme (APP) and, more recently, the pandemic emergency purchase programme (PEPP) as a sign that the ECB has started monetizing sovereign debt at the expense of its primary mandate of price stability." But these fears are unfounded, she argues: "First, there is no systematic relationship between government bond issuance and the amount of bonds that we purchase in the secondary market [...]. Rather, our measures aim to deliver financial conditions that are consistent with a return of inflation to our medium-term aim. Second, our monetary policy stance is not directly related to the level of sovereign debt."

Others are more worried. For instance, Bartsch *et al.* (2020) refer in particular to *yield curve control* (YCC) as implemented by some central banks. Under YCC, the central bank commits to keep government bond yields close to a certain (low) level, thereby de facto forcing "the central bank to target the provision of additional policy space for the fiscal authority. In that sense, YCC could be interpreted as a soft form of (or an antechamber to) fiscal dominance." The Bank of Japan adopted YCC on 21 September 2016, while the Reserve Bank of Australia formally adopted YCC targeting in March 2020 and discontinued it in November 2021. The crucial difference with QE is that, under QE, the central bank sets the quantity of the assets to be purchased, while under YCC it sets the price of the assets. As a result, the size of the purchases becomes endogenous, depending on the government's debt issuance on the one hand and the market's willingness to hold the debt at the targeted yield level. According to Bartsch *et al.* (2020), due to government's political pressure, YCC is difficult to exit.

However, one may wonder whether this is so different from the position of central banks pursuing other strategies. Until recently, central banks were pursuing asset purchase programmes, with the aim of ensuring that inflation is consistent with their targets. If these policies would remain in place in the future for longer than is necessary from a price stability perspective, putting at risk that inflation expectations may even become unanchored, then the spectre of a regime of fiscal dominance may loom. Furthermore, central banks may be restrained in raising interest rates in view of the high level of government debt in many advanced economies.

4.5   GREENING CENTRAL BANK POLICIES

In August 2021, the UN's Intergovernmental Panel on Climate Change (IPCC)—an intergovernmental body for the advancement of knowledge on human-induced climate change—concluded in its sixth assessment report that there is overwhelming evidence that global temperatures are rising and that it is caused by human activities (see Figure 4.9). Moreover, the IPCC concluded that rising global temperatures are already contributing to an increase in extreme weather events around the world. To counter the threats of climate change, 196 countries signed the Paris Agreement in 2015, agreeing to keep the rise in average global temperatures to well below 2 degrees Celsius above pre-industrial levels and to limit the increase to 1.5 degrees. In its most recent report, the IPCC cautions that, unless urgent and significant cuts in the global emissions of greenhouse gasses are made, the objectives of the Paris Agreement will no longer be within reach.

Climate change is an important challenge for the global economy in the decades ahead. Subject to considerable uncertainty, the OECD (2015)

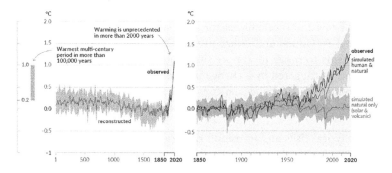

Figure 4.9   Average global surface temperatures compared with pre-industrial period

Source: IPCC (2021).

estimates that, if climate change is left to continue unabated, the rise in global temperatures will lower global GDP by 2–10 per cent in 2100. In addition, according to the OECD (2017), annual global investments amounting to USD 6.9 trillion until 2030 are necessary to limit global warming to 2 degrees Celsius above pre-industrial levels, or around 8 per cent of global GDP every year. This implies that investment needs to be considerably higher if countries want to live up to their commitment under the Paris Agreement of 2015 to limit global warming to well below 2 degrees Celsius. These figures illustrate that climate change will have a substantial impact on the global economy, both when it is addressed and when it is not addressed.

When analysing the consequences of climate change on the economy and the financial system, economists typically distinguish between physical risks and transition risks (BIS, 2021). Physical risks relate to the potential impact of climate change and extreme weather events on the economy, such as damages caused by increased precipitation, flooding and heatwaves. These events can negatively impact economic activity, while also harming incomes of individual households and firms and their ability to service their debts. Increased physical risks may also impact spending and investment patterns because economic agents need to adapt to the increased likelihood of experiencing hazards from extreme weather events and natural disasters. Transition risks relate to the potential economic and financial consequences of a transition to a sustainable economy in which emissions of greenhouse gasses are reduced to net zero. This may impact firms and economic sectors that are currently large contributors to global emissions and either need to be wound down or undertake investments to move to a more sustainable business model. Transition risks can be triggered by a change in legislation, e.g., implementation of a carbon tax, or by changes in consumer preferences in favour of goods and services that are more environmentally sustainable.

Both physical risks and transition risks can lead to the stranding of real and financial assets, negatively impacting the balance sheet of financial institutions. This implies that physical and transition risks of climate change constitute a source of financial risks that need to be managed by financial institutions as any other material risk that they face. More specifically, the BCBS recently concluded in a report prepared by a dedicated taskforce that climate-related financial risks can be captured in traditional financial risk categories, like credit risk, market risk, liquidity risk, operational risk and reputational risk (BIS, 2021). At the same time, considerable challenges remain in terms of reliably estimating the size of these risks, *inter alia* because of remaining data gaps and uncertainty with respect to how the physical and transition risks of climate change will ultimately materialize. Supervisors need to ascertain that financial institutions manage adequately all material risks, including climate-related and environmental risks.

Beyond the impact on the financial sector, climate change may also have macroeconomic implications that impact the conduct of monetary policy. The ECB (2021) identifies several potential mechanisms. First, climate change may exert further downward pressure on the equilibrium interest rate (see section 4.1), e.g., as a consequence of increased uncertainty about the economic outlook and an increase in general risk aversion. This may further exacerbate the incidence of policy rates hitting the effective lower bound. Second, climate risks can make it more difficult to assess the appropriate stance for monetary policy when it complicates the identification of shocks that hit the economy. In other words, climate change events may materialize and transmit throughout the economy in different ways from the shocks that central banks typically experience, complicating the assessment of the optimal policy response. Finally, the materialization of climate risks may also lead to more frequent and more pronounced shocks hitting the economy, adding to the volatility of economic activity and inflation to which monetary policy may need to respond in the pursuit of its mandate (Schnabel, 2022a).

The exact impact of climate risks on inflation and therefore monetary policy is uncertain and will depend on the extent to which the transition of the global economy to compatibility with the objectives of the Paris Agreement will be successful. Three potential mechanisms have been identified by Schnabel (2022b). First, there can be upward pressure on inflation due to an increase in the number of natural disasters and increased whether events (dubbed "climateflation"), for example increased food prices due to droughts. Second, as long as economies are still highly dependent on fossil-based energy sources, the increased scarcity of fossil fuels would put upward pressure on inflation ("fossilflation"). By contrast, the economy adjusting to the objectives of the Paris Agreement with companies investing in new green technologies may equally put upward pressure on inflation ("greenflation"). At the same time, a succesful green transition would limit the upward pressure on inflation that may come from "climateflation" and "fossilflation", underlining the uncertainty of the exact impact.

BOX 4.6 THE NETWORK OF CENTRAL BANKS AND SUPERVISORS FOR GREENING THE FINANCIAL SYSTEM

Recognizing that the physical and transition risks of climate change will have a major impact on the functioning of the economy and therefore also on the financial sector, eight central banks and supervisors joined forces in late 2017 to establish the Network of Central Banks and Supervisors for Greening the Financial System (NGFS). The NGFS serves to share best practices, to contribute to the development of environment and climate-risk management in the financial sector and to mobilize mainstream finance to support the transition of a sustainable economy. As of June 2022, the NGFS consists of 116 members and 19 observers covering 5 continents, and close to 90 per cent of the global economy.

The work of the NGFS covers all tasks and responsibilities of central banks and supervisors, including micro-prudential supervision, financial stability, own balance sheet management and monetary policy, and it has developed and shared practical tools and knowledge in all these fields. Notably, it has published a guide for the integration of climate-related and environmental risks in the supervision of banks, e.g., by communicating expectations on how supervisors expect banks to deal with these risks and engaging with banks in the regular supervisory dialogue. Moreover, the NGFS has produced jointly with a coalition from academia macroeconomic scenarios for climate change. These scenarios provide a framework for analysing the impact of physical and transition risks under different climate policy assumptions. While they have been developed for use by central banks and supervisors, they may also be useful for governments, academia and private sector entities. With these scenarios, the NGFS provides – and intends to regularly update – an important public good for all stakeholders, public and private, to help them engage in forward-looking climate-risk analysis under a common and consistent global reference framework.

In March 2021, the Network of Central Banks and Supervisors for Greening the Financial System (NGFS, see Box 4.6) released a report outlining options for central banks to adapt monetary policy operations to incorporate climate change considerations. The report concludes that—irrespective of there being a successful transition to a climate-neutral economy, or not—climate change and climate change policies expose central banks and the counterparties that they interact with when implementing monetary policy to financial risks. In extreme cases, climate-related shocks can even lead to distortions to a smooth implementation of monetary policy, impairing an effective pursuit of its mandate. To address these risks, the report includes several suggestions on how the implementation framework of monetary policy can be adapted to take incorporate climate-risk considerations, e.g., by amending credit operations, collateral policies and asset purchases. While the report makes no specific recommendations and leaves it for individual central banks to consider what options fit best their mandate and specific context, it does underline an emerging consensus among central banks that climate change has implications for the conduct of monetary policy.

As an example of a central bank acting in accordance with the suggestions provided in the NGFS report on monetary policy options, the ECB has announced its intention to implement a climate action plan to incorporate climate change considerations into its monetary policy framework. The climate action plan is part of the outcome of the ECB's strategy review that was concluded in July 2021 (see section 2.2). In its revised monetary policy strategy statement, the ECB recognizes that climate change will have profound implications for the ECB's primary objective of price stability through the impact on the structure and cyclical dynamics of the economy and the financial system. To account for this, the ECB will invest in expanding its analytical capabilities to incorporate climate change in macroeconomic modelling, statistics and its monetary policy assessments. Moreover, it set out preparatory work to amend its monetary policy operations to include climate change considerations by, *inter alia*, adding disclosure requirements as an eligibility criterium for collateral and asset purchases and including climate-risk considerations in collateral policies and asset purchase strategies. As argued by ECB Executive Board member Isabel Schnabel (2021), climate risks remain mispriced, implying the presence of negative externalities and market failures. This may warrant that central banks consider moving from a market-neutral benchmark for the implementation of monetary policy operations—i.e., a benchmark that reflects assets outstanding in the market, to a benchmark that better fosters a market efficient allocation of resources.

In November 2021, the BoE announced a specific approach to greening its Corporate Bond Purchase scheme. Whereas the total size of the corporate bond holdings continues to be guided by what is necessary to achieve the inflation target, the composition of the portfolio will be gradually adjusted to ensure consistency with the commitment of the UK government to move to a net zero greenhouse gas emissions economy by 2050. The new approach implies that the BoE will start imposing climate governance requirements as an eligibility criterion for the purchase of corporate bonds. Moreover, issuers with any coal mining activities will become ineligible. Using the information that corporate bond issuers need to disclose on their climate performance, the BoE will start tilting its purchases towards stronger performers. It will set out to intensify this approach over time, to ensure convergence over time with the government's commitment to net zero by 2050.

Whereas in policy circles steps are being undertaken to integrate climate-related and environmental risks into the core activities of central banks and supervisors, some academics have expressed their scepticism. For example, Nobel laureate Lars Peter Hansen (2021) argues that central banks should be careful so as not to overstate their understanding of the impact of climate change on the economy and the financial sector and their ability to mitigate its effects. Cochrane (2020) warns that central banks incorporating climate change considerations could be harmful for central bank independence and central banks' ability to pursue their objectives to control inflation and stem financial crises. In this context, it should be noted that the discussion focuses primarily on the scope that central banks and supervisors have to incorporate climate change considerations within their mandates. Among proponents and critics of action by central banks and supervisors there is no disagreement that governments are primarily responsible for taking climate action and setting climate policies.

NOTES

1. As the general price level increases over time, anybody lending a sum of money must bear in mind that the same sum, when it is repaid, will have lost value. The *real interest rate*, which is roughly equal to the interest rate minus average inflation over the loan's maturity period, is therefore a better measure of the cost of borrowing.
2. Recent research has proposed that the long-run Phillips curve for growth and inflation could even be downward-sloping, i.e., higher inflation being associated with lower growth in the long run (Ascari *et al.*, 2022).
3. The Chicago Board Options Exchange's equity option volatility index (VIX) is often used as indicator of risk appetite, where lower values indicate a greater tolerance for risk-taking.
4. This section heavily draws on Bartsch *et al.* (2020).
5. This does not hold for so-called automatic fiscal stabilizers, which work in real time and do not require deliberate decisions. For instance, social transfers designed to protect against economic downturns (e.g., unemployment benefits) work countercyclically: the unemployed receive support so that they do not need to cut their spending, which would deepen the recession.
6. When public debt matures, most often the principal amount is paid back by issuing new debt.

References

Adrian, T. (2018). Challenges for Monetary Policy from Global Financial Cycles. Opening Speech of the IMF/SNB Conference. https://www.imf.org/en/News/Articles/2018/05/07/sp050818-challenges-for-monetary-policy-from-global-financial-cycles

Alesina, A., F. Campante and G. Tabellini (2008). Why Is Fiscal Policy often Procyclical? *Journal of the European Economic Association*, 6(5), 1006–1036.

Ascari, G., P. Bonomolo and Q. Haque (2022). The Long-Run Phillips Curve Is … A Curve. Working Paper. Available at: https://sites.google.com/site/guidoascari/working-papers.

Bagehot, W. (1873). *Lombard Street. A Description of the Money Market.* London, Henry S. King.

Banerjee, S., and M.S. Mohanty (2021). US Monetary Policy and the Financial Channel of the Exchange Rate: Evidence from India. BIS Working Paper 945.

Baqaee, D., and E. Fahri (2020). Supply and Demand in Disaggregated Keynesian Economies with an Application to the COVID-19 Crisis. NBER Working Paper 27152.

Bartsch, E., A. Bénassy-Quéré, G. Corsetti and X. Debrun (2020). It's All in the Mix. How Monetary and Fiscal Policies Can Work or Fail Together. Geneva Reports on the World Economy 23, Geneva, ICMBS/London, CEPR.

Bernanke, B.S. (2004). The Great Moderation. Remarks at the meeting of the Eastern Economic Association, Washington D.C., United States, 20 February.

Bernanke, B.S. (2010). Central Bank Independence, Transparency, and Accountability. Speech at the Institute for Monetary and Economic Studies International Conference, Bank of Japan, Tokyo, Japan, 25 May, https://www.federalreserve.gov/newsevents/speech/bernanke20100525a.htm.

Bernanke, B.S. (2013). Communication and Monetary Policy. Herbert Stein Memorial Lecture. https://www.federalreserve.gov/newsevents/speech/bernanke20131119a.htm.

Bernanke, B.S. (2015a). *The Courage to Act. A Memoir of a Crisis and Its Aftermath.* London, W.W. Norton & Company.

Bernanke, B.S. (2015b). The Taylor Rule: A Benchmark for Monetary Policy? https://www.brookings.edu/blog/ben-bernanke/2015/04/28/the-taylor-rule-a-benchmark-for-monetary-policy/.

BIS (2016). Annual Report 2016. Basle, Bank for International Settlements.

BIS (2020). Annual Report 2020. Basle, Bank for International Settlements.

BIS (2021). Basel Committee on Banking Supervision. Climate-Related Risk Drivers and Their Transmission Channels. Basle, Bank for International Settlements. https://www.bis.org/bcbs/publ/d517.pdf.

Blinder, A.S. (2004). *The Quiet Revolution. Central Banking Goes Modern.* New Haven, Yale University Press.

Blinder, A. (2007). Monetary Policy by Committee. Why and How? *European Journal of Political Economy*, 23(1), 106–123.

Blinder, A.S., M. Ehrmann, M. Fratzscher, J. de Haan and D. Jansen (2008). Central Bank Communication and Monetary Policy: A Survey of Theory and Evidence. *Journal of Economic Literature*, 46, 910–945.

Blinder, A.S., M. Ehrmann, J. de Haan and D. Jansen (2017). Necessity as the Mother of Invention: Monetary Policy after the Crisis. *Economic Policy*, 32(92), 707–755.

Bodea, C., and R. Hicks (2015). Price Stability and Central Bank Independence. Discipline, Credibility and Democratic Institutions. *International Organization*, 69(1), 35–61.

Bonam, D., P. van Els, J.W. van den End, L. de Haan and I. Hindrayanto (2018). The Natural Rate of Interest from a Monetary and Financial Perspective. DNB Occasional Study 16-3.

Bonam, D., G. Galati, I. Hindrayanto, M. Hoeberichts, A. Samarina and I. Stanga (2019). Inflation in the Euro Area since the Global Financial Crisis. DNB Occasional Study, 17-3.

Bonam, D., J. de Haan and D. van Limbergen (2021a). Time-varying Wage Phillips Curves in the Euro Area with a New Measure for Labor Market Slack. *Economic Modelling*, 96, 157–171.

Bonam, D., J. de Haan and B. Soederhuizen (2021b). The Effects of Fiscal Policy at the Effective Lower Bound. *Macroeconomic Dynamics*, 26(1), 149–185.

Bonam, D., and A. Smadu (2021). The Long-Run Effects of Pandemics on Inflation: Will This Time Be Different? *Economic Letters*, 208, 1–4.

Bordo, M.D., and P.L. Siklos (2018). Central Banks: Evolution and Innovation in Historical Perspective. In: Edvinsson, R., Jacobson, T. and Waldenström, D. (eds.), *Sveriges Riksbank and the History of Central Banking*. Cambridge, Cambridge University Press, pp. 26–89.

Borio, C.E.V., and P. Disyatat (2010). Unconventional Monetary Policies: An Appraisal. *The Manchester School*, 78(1), 53–89.

Borio, C., M. Erdem, A. Filardo and B. Hofmann (2015). The Costs of Deflations: A Historical Perspective. *BIS Quarterly Review*, March, 31–54.

Borio, C., M. Juselius, P. Disyatat and M. Drehmann (2017). Monetary Policy, the Financial Cycle, and Ultra-Low Interest Rates. *International Journal of Central Banking*, 13(3), 55–89.

Borio, C., and W.R. White (2004). Whither Monetary and Financial Stability? The Implications of Evolving Policy Regimes. BIS Working Paper 147.

Borrallo Egea, F., and P. del Río López (2021). Monetary Policy Strategy and Inflation in Japan. Banco de España Working Paper 2116.

Brunnermeier, M.K., and Y. Koby (2018). The Reversal Interest Rate. NBER Working Paper 25406.

Buiter, W.H. (2003). Deflation: Prevention and Cure. NBER Working Paper 9623.

Calomiris, C.W., M. Flandreau and L. Laeven (2016). Political Foundations of the Lender of Last Resort: A Global Historical Narrative. *Journal of Financial Intermediation*, 28, 48–65.

Carney, M. (2015). How Is Inflation Affected by Globalisation? Remarks by the Governor of the Bank of England, World Economic Forum, Jackson Hole, WY, 29 August.

Cerutti, E., S. Claessens and A.K. Rose (2017). How Important Is the Global Financial Cycle? Evidence from Capital Flows. IMF Working Paper 17/193.

Cerutti, E., R. Correa, E. Fiorentino and E. Segalla (2015). Changes in Prudential Policy Instruments – A New Cross Country Database. *International Journal of Central Banking*, 48, 477–503.

Chinn, M.D., and H. Ito (2006). What Matters for Financial Development? Capital Controls, Institutions, and Interactions. *Journal of Development Economics*, 81(1), 163–192.

Christiano, L.J., M. Eichenbaum and M. Trabandt (2015). Understanding the Great Recession. *American Economic Journal: Macroeconomics*, 7(1), 110–167.

Ciccarelli, M., and C. Osbat (2017). Low Inflation in the Euro Area: Causes and Consequences. ECB Occasional Paper 181.

Cochrane, J.H. (2020). Central Banks and Climate: A Case of Mission Creep. https://www.hoover.org/research/central-banks-and-climate-case-mission-creep

Coibion, O., and Y. Gorodnichenko (2015). Is the Phillips Curve Alive and Well After All? Inflation Expectations and the Missing Disinflation. *American Economic Journal: Macroeconomics*, 7(1), 197–232.

Colciago, A., A. Samarina and J. de Haan (2019). Central Bank Policies and Income and Wealth Inequality: A Survey. *Journal of Economic Surveys*, 33(4), 1199–1231.

Conti-Brown, P. (2015). The Twelve Federal Reserve Banks: Governance and Accountability in the 21st Century. Hutchins Center of Monetary and Fiscal Policy at Brookings, Working Paper 10.

Corsello, F., S. Neri and A. Tagliabracci (2021). Anchored or De-anchored? That is the Question. *European Journal of Political Economy*, 69, art. 102031.

Cukierman, A., S.B. Webb and B. Neyapti (1992). Measuring the Independence of Central Banks and Its Effects on Policy Outcomes. *The World Bank Economic Review*, 6, 353–398.

Daly, M., B. Hobijn and B. Lucking (2012). Why Wage Growth Stayed Strong? *Federal Reserve Bank of San Francisco Economic Letter*, 10, 2 April.

de Haan, J. (2018). The Struggle of German Central Banks to Maintain Price Stability. In: Edvinsson, R., Jacobson, T. and Waldenström, D. (eds.), *Sveriges Riksbank and the History of Central Banking*. Cambridge, Cambridge University Press, pp. 388–417.

de Haan, J., C. Bodea, R. Hicks and S.C.W. Eijffinger (2018). Central Bank Independence Before and After the Crisis. *Comparative Economic Studies*, 60(2), 182–202.

de Haan, J., S.C.W. Eijffinger and S. Waller (2005). *The European Central Bank: Credibility, Transparency, and Centralization*. Cambridge (MA), MIT Press.

de Haan, J., R. Inklaar and R. Jong-A-Pin (2008). Will Business Cycles in the Euro Area Converge? A Critical Survey of Empirical Research. *Journal of Economic Surveys*, 22, 234–273.

de Haan, J., D. Schoenmaker and P. Wierts (2020). *Financial Markets and Institutions: A European Perspective* (fourth edition). Cambridge, Cambridge University Press.

de Haan, J., and J.-E. Sturm (2019). Central Bank Communication: How To Manage Expectations? In: Mayes, D., Siklos, P. and Sturm, J.-E. (eds.), *The Oxford Handbook of the Economics of Central Banking*. Oxford, Oxford University Press, pp. 231–262.

Den Haan, W. (ed.) (2013). *Forward Guidance: Perspectives from Central Bankers, Scholars and Market Participants*. VoxEU e-book. London, CEPR.

Deutsche Bundesbank (1995). *The Monetary Policy of the Bundesbank*. Frankfurt am Main, Deutsche Bundesbank.

Deutsche Bundesbank (2017). The Role of Banks, Non-banks and the Central Bank in the Money Creation Process. Deutsche Bundesbank Monthly Report, April.

Dincer, N.N., and B. Eichengreen (2014). Central Bank Transparency and Independence: Updates and New Measures. *International Journal of Central Banking*, 10(1), 189–253.

ECB (2021). Climate Change and Monetary Policy in the Euro Area. ECB Occasional Paper 271. Frankfurt am Main, European Central Bank. https://www.ecb.europa.eu/pub/pdf/scpops/ecb.op271~36775d43c8.en.pdf.

Edge, R.M., and J.N. Liang (2019). New Financial Stability Governance Structures and Central Banks. Hutchins Center Working Paper 50.

Edge, R.M., and J.N. Liang (2020). Financial Stability Governance and Basel III Macroprudential Capital Buffers. Hutchins Center Working Paper 56.

Eichengreen, B. (2018). The Two Eras of Central Banking in the United States. In: Edvinsson, R., Jacobson, T. and Waldenström, D. (eds.), *Sveriges Riksbank and the History of Central Banking*. Cambridge, Cambridge University Press, pp. 361–387.

Eijffinger, S.C.W., and P. Geraats (2006). How Transparent Are Central Banks? *European Journal of Political Economy*, 22(1), 1–22.

Enria, A. (2021). Basel III Implementation: The Last Mile Is Always the Hardest. Speech at the Marco Fanno Alumni online conference, Frankfurt am Main, 3 May. https://www.bankingsupervision.europa.eu/press/speeches/date/2021/html/ssm.sp210503~1672b8b1f0.en.html.

Forbes, K.J. (2019). Has Globalization Changed the Inflation Process? BIS Working Paper 896.

Galati, G., and R. Moessner (2018). What Do We Know about the Effectiveness of Macroprudential Policy. *Economica*, 85(340), 735–770.

Ghosh, A.R., M.S. Qureshi, J.I. Kim and J. Zalduendo (2014). Surges. *Journal of International Economics*, 92, 266–285.

Gilchrist, S., R. Schoenle, J.W. Sim and E. Zakrajsek (2015). Inflation Dynamics during the Financial Crisis. Finance and Economics Discussion Series, 2015-12, Board of Governors of the Federal Reserve System.

Goodhart, C. (2018). The Bank of England, 1694–2017. In: Edvinsson, R., Jacobson, T. and Waldenström, D. (eds.), *Sveriges Riksbank and the History of Central Banking*. Cambridge, Cambridge University Press, pp. 143–171.

Goodhart, C., and M. Pradhan (2020). The Great Demographic Reversal: Ageing Societies, Waning Inequality, and an Inflation Revival. SUERF Policy Note 197.

Goodhart, C., and D. Schoenmaker (1995). Should the Functions of Monetary Policy and Banking Supervision Be Separated? *Oxford Economic Papers*, 47(4), 539–560.

Gorter J., J. Jacobs and J. de Haan (2008). Taylor Rules for the ECB Using Expectations Data. *The Scandinavian Journal of Economics*, 110(3), 473–488.

Greider, W. (1989). *Secrets of the Temple. How the Federal Reserve Runs the Country*. New York, Simon & Schuster.

Gros, D., and D. Schoenmaker (2014). European Deposit Insurance and Resolution in the Banking Union. *Journal of Common Market Studies*, 52, 529–546.

Ha, J., M.A. Kose and F. Ohnsorge (2019). *Inflation in Emerging and Developing Economies. Evolution, Drivers and Policies.* World Bank Group, Washington DC.

Habib, M.M., and F. Venditti (2018). The Global Financial Cycle. Implications for the Global Economy and the Euro Area. ECB Economic Bulletin, Issue 6/2018.

Haldane, A. (2017). A Little More Conversation, A Little Less Action. Speech given at the Federal Reserve Bank of San Francisco's Macroeconomics and Monetary Policy Conference, 31 March. https://www.bankofengland.co.uk/speech/2017/a-little-more-conversation-a-little-less-action.

Hansen, L.P. (2021). Central Banking Challenges Posed by Uncertain Climate Change and Natural Disasters. *Journal of Monetary Economics*, forthcoming. https://doi.org/10.1016/j.jmoneco.2021.09.010

Hartmann, P., and F. Smets (2018). The First Twenty Years of the European Central Bank. Monetary Policy. CEPR Discussion Paper 13411.

Hindrayanto, I., A. Samarina and I.M. Stanga (2019). Is the Phillips Curve Still Alive? Evidence from the Euro Area. *Economics Letters*, 174, 149–152.

Holston, K., T. Laubach and J.C. Williams (2017). Measuring the Natural Rate of Interest: International Trends and Determinants. *Journal of International Economics*, 108, S59–S75.

IPCC (2021). Sixth Assessment Report. https://www.ipcc.ch/report/ar6/wg1/#FullReport.

Irwin, N. (2013). *The Alchemists: Three Central Bankers and a World on Fire.* London, Penguin.

Issing, O. (2008). *The Birth of the Euro.* Cambridge, Cambridge University Press.

Jašová, M., R. Moessner and E. Takáts (2018). Domestic and Global Output Gaps as Inflation Drivers: What Does the Phillips Curve Tell? BIS Working Paper 748.

Kamber, G., M. Mohanty and J. Morley (2020). Have the Driving Forces of Inflation Changed in Advanced and Emerging Market Economies? BIS Working Paper 791.

Keister, T. (2018). Corridors and Floors in Monetary Policy. Liberty Street Economics. https://libertystreeteconomics.newyorkfed.org/2012/04/corridors-and-floors-in-monetary-policy/.

King, M. (2021). The King Canute Theory of Inflation. https://www.bloomberg.com/opinion/articles/2021-11-24/central-banks-should-abandon-the-king-canute-theory-of-inflation.

Klomp, J., and J. de Haan (2010). Inflation and Central Bank Independence: A Meta Regression Analysis. *Journal of Economic Surveys*, 24(4), 593–621.

Kohn, D.L. (2010). Federal Reserve's Policy Actions during the Financial Crisis and Lessons for the Future. Speech. https://www.bis.org/review/r100517d.pdf.

Kuroda, H. (2013). Overcoming Deflation and After. Speech at the Meeting of Nippon Keidanren (Japan Business Federation) in Tokyo. https://www.boj.or.jp/en/announcements/press/koen_2013/data/ko131225a1.pdf

Kuttner, K.N., and P.C. Mosser (2002). The Monetary Transmission Mechanism: Some Answers and Further Questions. FRBNY Economic Policy Review, May, 15–26.

Laeven, L. (2016). Speech at the SUERF Colloquium and Deutsche Bundesbank conference The SSM at 1. Frankfurt, 3 February. https://www.suerf.org/docx/l_e2c420d928d4bf8ce0ff2ec19b371514_5323_suerf.pdf.

Lundvall, H. (2020). What Is Driving the Global Trend towards Lower Real Interest Rates? *Sveriges Riksbank Economic Review*, 2020(1), 105–121.

Marsh, D. (1992). *The Bundesbank. The Bank That Rules Europe*. London, Heinemann.

Masciandaro, D., and D. Romelli (2018). Central Bankers as Supervisors: Do Crises Matter? *European Journal of Political Economy*, 52, 120–140.

Meltzer, A.H. (2010). *A History of the Federal Reserve, Vol. 2: 1970–1986.* Chicago, University of Chicago Press.

Miranda-Agrippino, S., and H. Rey (2020). US Monetary Policy and the Global Financial Cycle. *The Review of Economic Studies*, 87(6), 2754–2776.

Mishkin, F.S. (2017). Rethinking Monetary Policy after the Crisis. *Journal of International Money and Finance*, 73, 252–274.

Moessner, R., D. Jansen and J. de Haan (2017). Communication about Future Policy Rates in Theory and Practice. A Survey. *Journal of Economic Surveys*, 31(3), 678–711.

Obstfeld, M. (2015). Trilemmas and Tradeoffs. Living with Financial Globalisation. BIS Working Paper 480.

Obstfeld, M. (2020). Global Dimensions of U.S. Monetary Policy. *International Journal of Central Banking*, 16(1), 73–132.

Obstfeld, M., and A.M. Taylor (2017). International Monetary Relations: Taking Finance Seriously. *Journal of Economic Perspectives*, 31(3), 3–28.

OECD (2015). Climate Change Mitigation. Policies and Progress. Paris, OECD. https://www.oecd.org/env/climate-change-mitigation-9789264238787-en.htm.

OECD (2017). Investing in Climate. Investing in Growth. Paris, OECD. https://www.oecd.org/env/investing-in-climate-investing-in-growth-9789264273528-en.htm.

Phillips, A.W. (1958). The Relation between Unemployment and the Rate of Change of Money Wage Rates in the United Kingdom 1861–1957. *Economica*, 25(100), 283–299.

Reinhart, C.M., and V.R. Reinhart (2010). After the Fall. In: Federal Reserve Bank of Kansas City, Economic Policy Symposium, Macroeconomic Challenges: The Decade Ahead at Jackson Hole, Wyoming, 26–28 August.

Rey, H. (2013). Dilemma not Trilemma: The Global Financial Cycle and Monetary Policy Independence. In: *Proceedings of the 2013 Jackson Hole Symposium*, pp. 285–333.

Rogoff, K. (1985). The Optimal Degree of Commitment to an Intermediate Monetary Target. *Quarterly Journal of Economics*, 100(November), 1169–1189.

Rose, A. (2017). The Global Financial Cycle. Closer to an Anticlimax than a Juggernaut. VoxEU, August 14.

Schnabel, I. (2020). The Shadow of Fiscal Dominance. Misconceptions, Perceptions and Perspectives. SUERF Policy Note Issue 198.

Schnabel, I. (2021). From Market Neutrality to Market Efficiency. Welcome address at the ECB DG-Research Symposium "Climate change, financial markets and green growth". https://www.ecb.europa.eu/press/key/date/2021/html/ecb.sp210614~162bd7c253.en.html

Schnabel, I. (2022a). Looking through Higher Energy Prices? Monetary Policy and the Green Transition. Remarks at a panel on "Climate and the Financial System" at the American Finance Association 2022 Virtual Annual Meeting. https://www.ecb.europa.eu/press/key/date/2022/html/ecb.sp220108~0425a24eb7.en.html.

Schnabel, I. (2022b). A new age of energy inflation: climateflation, fossilflation and greenflation. Speech at a panel on "Monetary Policy and Climate Change" at the ECB and its Watchers XXII Conference. https://www.ecb.europa.eu/press/key/date/2022/html/ecb.sp220317_2~dbb3582f0a.en.html.

Summers, L.H. (2014). US Economic Prospects: Secular Stagnation, Hysteresis, and the Zero Lower Bound. *Business Economics*, 49(2), 65–73.

Svensson, L.E.O. (1997). Inflation Forecast Targeting. Implementing and Monitoring Inflation Targets. *European Economic Review*, 41(6), 1111–1146.

Svensson, L.E.O. (2003). What is Wrong with Taylor Rules? Using Judgment in Monetary Policy through Targeting Rules. *Journal of Economic Literature*, 41, 427–477.

Svensson, L.E.O. (2006). The Instrument-Rate Projection under Inflation Targeting. The Norwegian Example. In: *Proceedings of the Conference to Commemorate the 80th Anniversary of Banco de Mexico*, "Stability and Economic Growth: The Role of the Central Bank", pp.175–198.

Svensson, L.E.O. (2016). A Simple Cost–Benefit Analysis of Using Monetary Policy for Financial-Stability Purposes. In: Blanchard, O.J., Rajan, R., Rogoff, K.S. and Summers, L.H. (eds.), *Progress and Confusion: The State of Macroeconomic Policy*. Cambridge (MA), MIT Press, pp. 107-118..

Taylor, J.B. (1993). Discretion versus Policy Rules in Practice. *Carnegie-Rochester Conference Series on Public Policy*, 39, 195–214.

Wieland, V., and M. Wolters (2013). Forecasting and Policy Making. In: Elliott, G., and Timmermann, A. (eds.), *Handbook of Economic Forecasting*, vol. 2A, Elsevier, Amsterdam, pp. 239–325.

Williams, J.C. (2018a). Remarks at the 42nd Annual Central Banking Seminar. https://www.bis.org/review/r181003c.pdf.

Yellen, J.L. (2014). Monetary Policy and Financial Stability. The 2014 Michel Camdessus Central Banking Lecture, International Monetary Fund, 2 June.

Index

Titles in the **Elgar Advanced Introductions** series include: